David Young taught music history and theory at the Royal Northern College of Music, worked for the Associated Board of the Royal Schools of Music as a consultant in South East Asia, and was Professor of Performance Studies at Kampala University and Vice-Chancellor of the East Africa University, Rwanda.

He is editor of *Haydn the Innovator: A New Approach to the String Quartets* (2000) and author of *Beethoven Symphonies Revisited: Performance, Expression and Impact* (2021) and his scholarly writings have appeared in the *RMA Research Chronicle, Current Musicology, New Grove Dictionary of Music and Musicians*, and the *International Haydn Symposium*.

To Sally and Emily

David Young

READING ELGAR'S
THE MUSIC MAKERS

AUSTIN MACAULEY PUBLISHERS®

LONDON • CAMBRIDGE • NEW YORK • SHARJAH

A CIP catalogue record for this title is available from the British Library.

ISBN 9781035853274 (Paperback)
ISBN 9781035853281 (ePub e-book)

www.austinmacauley.com

First Published 2024
Austin Macauley Publishers Ltd®
1 Canada Square
Canary Wharf
London
E14 5AA

Several scholars and colleagues have helped me in various ways. Friends, especially in The Elgar Society, have engaged with the subject either by listening to my presentations and offering invaluable feedback or engaging in conversation and sharing ideas. Arthur Reynolds shared both ideas and materials, including the printed programme for the Birmingham premiere of Elgar's Ode. Bernard Porter was kind enough to help with the political, social, and historical context for Elgar's attitudes in certain matters around 1912. Meinhard Saremba provided helpful information about Elgar's knowledge of Gilbert and Sullivan operettas. Paul Grafton provided unique insight into Elgar's health issues when living at Severn House. Duncan Eves shared several stimulating thoughts about Wagner's influence on Elgar's music in general and *The Music Makers* in particular. I am also grateful to Chris Bennett, formerly of the Elgar Birthplace Museum (now The Firs), for kindly and generously preparing a digital copy of all the newspaper cuttings of press reviews of *The Music Makers* formerly preserved at the Birthplace Museum. With similar generosity, John Norris provided me with a complete list of Elgar's sketches for *The Music Makers* and an electronic copy of the late Martin Bird's unpublished transcriptions of Alice Elgar's diary entries for 1911, 1912 and 1913. Andrew Neill kindly read a draft of Chapter 1 (Introduction) and offered invaluable comments and suggestions. Richard Westwood-Brookes kindly read a draft of Chapter 2 (Reading the Critics) and offered helpful suggestions and encouragement. Jordan Kistler, author of a recent definitive study of O'Shaughnessy, kindly read a draft of Chapter 3 (Reading the Poetry) and offered encouragement and suggestions. Julian Rushton kindly read a draft of Chapter 4 (Reading the Music), the most substantial chapter, with meticulous attention to detail and offered invaluable suggestions. Caroline Gilderdale also reviewed Chapter 4 in a most helpful and supportive manner; in addition, Caroline carried out significant research on my behalf into the performance history of *The Music Makers* at The Three Choirs festivals.

Needless to say, none of the above can be held responsible in the slightest for any shortcomings in this short monograph.

Several libraries have provided immeasurable help and assistance. Chris Scobie of the British Library, London, arranged matters so that I could study all Elgar's sketches for *The Music Makers*, as well as the autograph vocal score, first edition, and proof-sheets. Susan Worrall, Director of Special Collections at the Cadbury Research Library, University of Birmingham, and her staff arranged for me to study the autograph full score and offered numerous kindnesses during my visit. Staff of the British Library, Boston Spa, showed endless patience, good humour, and helpfulness during my frequent visits, and the staff of the Public Library, Harrogate, were invariably welcoming during my occasional visits.

The musical examples are reproduced by kind permission of ©Hal Leonard Europe Ltd.

Analytical References

References to 'figures' refer to the rehearsal figures in both the orchestral score and the vocal score. Numbers after the figures are used as follows: figure 67.7 means the seventh bar after figure 67, etc.

In the analytical tables, including the Listener's Analytical Guide (Appendix 3), capital letters are used for major keys and lower case for minor keys.

Table of Contents

Chapter 1
Introduction

Three Hypotheses[1]

Writing about *The Music Makers*, op. 69, in 1968, Michael Kennedy felt the need to defend Elgar's Ode: '"Tinsel" and "tawdry" have been the pejorative words applied to this cantata, but rather than finding it "under-composed", I find it an original treatment of the poem, and one of Elgar's most endearing and unjustly under-rated works.'[2] Discussing the work as recently as 2020 and 2022, two speakers still felt the need to defend the work: 'After reading the poem, the score, and press reviews, one is left wondering why Elgar's *The Music Makers* at first met with such a muted response.'[3]

---

[1] I use the word hypothesis or hypotheses in the sense of an open investigation which looks beyond, and consequently challenges, received opinion, especially concerning critical reception, poetry and musical innovation.

[2] Michael Kennedy, *Portrait of Elgar* (Oxford University Press, 1968), p. 212.

[3] Elgar Society Yorkshire & North East Branch advertisement for a talk given on 25 January 2020 by David Young, Chairman of the Branch.

'Elgar's setting of Arthur O'Shaughnessy's "Ode" has been the subject of frequent critical maulings. A fresh look is needed at this under-rated masterpiece.'[4]

Why is it that with greater assurance than with perhaps any other work by Elgar, one can predict some kind of defence when *The Music Makers* is being written or spoken about in recent times, and is it reasonable to continue to describe the work as under-rated? With these thoughts in mind, this short handbook at its heart presents and tests three hypotheses: firstly, that Elgar's *The Music Makers* has experienced a chequered reputation; secondly, that part of the perceived problem has been with the poem by Arthur O'Shaughnessy; and, thirdly, that Elgar's setting represents a more innovatory artistic creation than is usually recognised.

The first hypothesis is tested, primarily in Chapter 2, by means of an examination of the critical reception within the first six months of the work's performances, a flavour of the history of concert performances as represented by the annual Promenade Concerts and Three Choirs Festivals, and evaluations in a range of books and scholarly articles. The second is tested, primarily in Chapter 3, by placing O'Shaughnessy's Ode in its historical and aesthetic context and discussing its strengths as a text for musical setting and its appeal for Elgar. The third, as tested primarily in Chapter 4, involves an exploration of Elgar's *modus operandi* in respect of melody, rhythm, use of voices, orchestration and tonality—in short, those elements which combine to produce the work's structure—in order to test whether Elgar's chief

---

[4] Elgar Society Southern Branch advertisement for a talk given on 19 March 2022 by Duncan Eves, Vice Chairman of the Branch.

innovation, the use of borrowed material, is supported and successfully integrated in the work as a whole. Although these three hypotheses lie at the heart of this monograph, they do not entirely define or restrict what can be examined or discussed if additional material is likely to illuminate further the nature of Elgar's setting.

'A Listener's Guide to *The Music Makers*' is included in the appendices; this brings together all the analytical elements discussed in Chapter 4 and may prove useful as an aid when listening to the work.

Sketches

Like Beethoven, Elgar was an inveterate sketcher of musical ideas, sometimes written whilst outdoors. Elgar's earliest sketches appear to have originated whilst accompanying his father by horse and trap to or from piano-tuning engagements; others may have been jotted down whilst sitting by the reed beds of the Severn, or elsewhere outdoors—but the actual business of composing with the aid of sketches was, of course, undertaken indoors: in music rooms, studies or hotel rooms. Again like Beethoven, Elgar preserved his sketches, or occasionally gave manuscript leaves to friends, especially Alice Stuart Wortley. The importance Elgar attached to the sketching process is evidenced by his ordering eight, elaborate, expensive sketchbooks from Novello's, through the offices of his friend and confidant August Jaeger, as sardonically described in

Elgar's annotation on a fly-leaf: 'Old Daddy Jaeger had these Books made for me—(I paid for them) alas!'[5]

In connection with *The Music Makers*, the earliest sketches, dating from around 1900, were originally intended for *The Dream of Gerontius*.[6] Further sketches were made intermittently, but especially in 1908, and during the spring of 1909 (whilst on holiday in Careggi, near Florence). Once work began in earnest, in early January 1912, Elgar continued sketching as well as returning to earlier sketchbooks.

The sketchbooks provide valuable evidence of the compositional process.[7] Such features will be discussed as they arise, but we can touch on several significant aspects immediately, such as evolving thoughts about the main key of the Ode, for the unusual choice of F minor did not occur immediately—in one sketch the first theme is annotated in C minor (which is presumably what Elgar had in mind at that point in the compositional process for the Ode as a whole);[8]

---

[5] London, British Library, Add. MS. 63156.

[6] London, British Library, Add. MS. 47902.

[7] Some of the sketchbooks relevant to *The Music Makers* were preserved at the Birthplace Museum (now The Firs) and others, especially those bequeathed by Carice Elgar Blake, at the British Museum. All are now preserved at the British Library, London. A complete list is given in the Bibliography. Detailed descriptions of the various sketches can be found in Robert Anderson and Jerrold Northrop Moore (eds), *The Music Makers, The Spirit of England, With Proud Thanksgiving*, Elgar Compete Edition, vol. 10 (London and Sevenoaks: Novello, 1986), pp. v-xxix, although it should be noted that references to locations were made prior to the gathering together of all these materials at the British Library.

[8] London, British Library, MS. Mus. 1843/1/6, f. 6.

early thoughts about the orchestral gesture leading to 'Great hail!' (figure 85); and the process leading to the placement of the arresting chord just before the end (figure 103). An advanced sketch of the two main themes of the orchestral introduction (in short score)—but without the unison crescendo at the very beginning—and headed 'the complete understanding', with the description 'climax' written against the ninth bar of the second theme (figure 2.8), provides valuable evidence of Elgar's method of composing, as described by his friend W.H. (Billy) Reed: 'He worked at a theme and brought it to a climax; for then, as he said to me, he knew to what he was leading.'[9]

Some Major Works Before *The Music Makers*

By the time of *The Music Makers*, Elgar, aged 55, was at the height of his career, with a catalogue of great music to his name, including orchestral works—the *'Enigma' Variations*, *'Cockaigne' Overture*, *Introduction and Allegro*, and two symphonies—the orchestrally-accompanied song cycle *Sea Pictures*, choral works—*The Dream of Gerontius*, *The Apostles*, *The Kingdom*—and the Violin Concerto. All these works date from a twelve-year period from 1899 and represent (setting aside the later chamber music and Cello Concerto) his most celebrated music. However, before the international success of the *'Enigma' Variations*, Elgar had composed and performed a number of large-scale works which had brought him to at least national attention, especially the concert overture *Froissart* (1890), the *Serenade*

---

[9] William H. Reed, *Elgar as I Knew Him* (London: Victor Gollancz, 1936), p. 129.

in E minor (1893), *The Black Knight* (1893), *The Light of Life (Lux Christi*, 1896), *King Olaf* (1896), and *Caractacus* (1898).

The Black Knight, op. 25—a setting of a ballad by Ludwig Uhland, translated by Henry Wadsworth Longfellow—has certain features in common with *The Music Makers*, especially their links, at least in the composer's mind, to symphonic form. In a letter to Jaeger (August 1898), Elgar described *The Black Knight* as 'a sort of symphony' and in the reprinted vocal score (1898) the composer went even further by describing it as 'a Symphony for Chorus and Orchestra'.[10] On the title page of the manuscript vocal score of the later work, as described below, Elgar tried out a similar description but eventually decided on calling it simply *The Music Makers*.[11] Elgar divided the text of the earlier work into four scenes, and these correspond to a certain extent to four movements of a symphony, and the use of orchestra and choral voices calls to mind certain symphonic procedures, as does some of the tonal organisation.[12] Similar conclusions can be drawn about *The Music Makers,* but formulating a convincing case for the work as a symphony *per se* is even

---

[10] Julian Rushton, '"How strange": Elgar's Early Notation for *The Black Knight*', *The Elgar Society Journal*, 22/3 (2020), pp. 5–11; 'Ballads and Demons: a context for *The Black Knight*', *The Elgar Society Journal*, 22/4 (2021), pp. 5–12; '*The Black Knight*: Elgar's first Symphony?' *The Elgar Society Journal*, 22/5 (2021), pp. 5–15.

[11] London, British Library, Add. MS. 58,036.

[12] Prof. Rushton concludes his thorough analysis of *The Black Knight* by indicating that there are pros and cons in describing it as a symphony, but only pros for describing it as 'a sort of symphony'. See '*The Black Knight*: Elgar's first Symphony?'

more difficult to do than for *The Black Knight* (as will be discussed further in Chapter 4).

Caractacus, op. 35—with a libretto by H.A. Acworth—may have a connection with *The Music Makers* in that a martial rhythm (four semiquavers followed by a crochet)—depicting the British army marching at night and appearing many times in the opening pages—reappears in op. 69, between figures 26.4 and 27.1, after the words 'can trample a kingdom down', and again at figure 83 at the word 'die'. Elgar does not acknowledge this as one of his borrowings or quotations, and it may be that he was simply depicting drum beat through readily recognisable patterns, yet the link between the two works is unmistakable.[13]

The spirit of the *'Enigma' Variations*, op. 36—the work which sealed Elgar's national and international reputation, and which remains perhaps his most popular orchestral work—hangs over *The Music Makers* with unmistakable intensity. As will be discussed in Chapter 4, Elgar clearly felt a spiritual affinity between the two works, as evidenced by his Note (for Ernest Newman's programme note) that he had 'used the opening bars of the theme "Enigma" of the *Variations* because it expressed when written (in 1898) [his] sense of the loneliness of the artist as described in the first six lines of the Ode, and that it still…[embodied] that sense.'

The 'Enigma' theme occurs more frequently than any other 'borrowing', and the 'Nimrod' variation forms arguably the main climactic and deeply moving passage of both works. The affinity between the two, however, extends beyond the

---

[13] I am grateful to Michael Butterfield for drawing my attention to this link (email, 9 January 2023).

spiritual to the innovatory: the *Variations* was probably the first orchestral work to portray a real character in each of its variations (what Elgar called 'friends pictured within'), and *The Music Makers* was probably the first vocal/orchestral work to incorporate themes from other pieces throughout the composition (despite the limited debt to Richard Strauss's *Ein Heldenleben*—as will be discussed further in Chapter 4).

Sea Pictures, op. 37 (1899), consisting of five songs by various poets—'Sea Slumber' (a setting of a poem by Roden Noel), 'In Haven (Capri)' (Caroline Alice Elgar), 'Sabbath Morning at Sea' (Elizabeth Barrett Browning), 'Where Corals Lie' (Richard Garnett), 'The Swimmer' (Adam Lindsay Gordon)—probably represents one of Elgar's finest large-scale works to date, demonstrating an impressive sense of unity across the cycle, despite widely different poetic styles. In *The Music Makers,* Elgar quotes from an orchestral phrase in 'Sea Slumber', which appears after the words 'Hush thee, O my child' and several times subsequently in the earlier work, and which appears in the later one at the words 'Wandering by lone sea-breakers, And sitting by desolate streams.' The sense of sorrow in Noel's poem, which seems to represent a lament for a lost child, is movingly portrayed by Elgar in *Sea Pictures*, and the quotation also serves in op. 69 to portray the rise and fall of the sea, as well as to express the mood of sadness which hangs over much of the work.

Regarded by many as Elgar's greatest choral work, *The Dream of Gerontius*, op. 38 (1900)—with a text based on John Henry Newman's poem of the same name—is quoted from twice in *The Music Makers*: firstly, at the word 'dreams' in the opening choral sentence 'We are the music makers, And we are the dreamers of dreams' (where the very opening of

Gerontius is quoted in the orchestra); and, secondly, near the end, at the words 'And a singer who sings no more'—where in the oratorio, the words are 'Novissima hora est' ('My end is near'). Here the symbolism of an ending is obvious, as is probably a reference to Elgar's dear departed friend August Jaeger (as will be discussed further in Chapter 4).

The Apostles, op. 49 (1903) is quoted from briefly and symbolically at the point of the words 'There shall ye see Him' which becomes in the Ode figuration against the words 'our dreaming', perhaps signifying Elgar's belief that in dreams truth can be revealed as significantly as in our waking hours. The combination with other 'borrowed' themes at this point produces one of the most moving moments in the work (as will be discussed in Chapter 4). *The Apostles* has a further connection with *The Music Makers*, this time indirect, in that it contains an example of 'borrowed' material, or 'self-quotation', thereby pre-dating the device in *The Music Makers*: at the words 'and recov'ring of sight to the blind', shortly into the first choral entry, Elgar quotes from *The Light of Light*.[14]

The two symphonies—no. 1 in A flat, op. 55 (1908), and no. 2 in E flat, op. 63 (1911)—experienced differing fortunes: the First achieved phenomenal acclaim and success throughout the UK, Europe and North America, whereas the Second a more restrained response and had to await the end

---

[14] In a sense, the *Coronation Ode* contains an even earlier example of self-borrowing, the most extended in all Elgar, in that the finale, 'Land of Hope and Glory', is an arrangement for contralto soloist and orchestra, with words by Arthur Benson, of the Trio section of the *Pomp and Circumstance March* no. 1, op. 39 (1901).

of the First World War to achieve a more elevated position. Now the two works are rightly regarded equally as amongst the composer's greatest. As will be discussed in Chapter 4, Elgar quotes from both in *The Music Makers* with an effect which is beyond impressive.

The Violin Concerto in B minor, op. 61 (1910), is firmly established alongside the concertos of Beethoven, Mendelssohn, Brahms, Bruch, Tchaikovsky, Sibelius, and others, as one of the greatest, and certainly most original. It also represents one of the composer's most personal works, in which he 'shewed' himself. The quotations in *The Music Makers*, as will be further discussed in Chapter 4, are both highly personal and significant.

The Making of The Music Makers[15]

Elgar's interest in setting Arthur O'Shaughnessy's Ode (first published in 1874) came to the public attention in March 1904 in an article by Edward Baughan in *The Daily News*.[16] In the same month, Elgar discussed a possible setting with Henry Embleton, Secretary of the Leeds Choral Union, in the

---

[15] Chief sources for this section are Jerrold Northrop Moore, *Edward Elgar: A Creative Life* (Oxford University Press, 1987), especially pp. 621–667; Robert Anderson and Jerrold Northrop Moore (eds), *The Music Makers, The Spirit of England, With Proud Thanksgiving*, Elgar Compete Edition, pp. v-xi; and Alice Elgar's diaries for 1912

[16] *The Daily News*, 25 March 1904.

hope of securing a commission for the Leeds Festival;[17] although Embleton was enthusiastic, this particular Leeds project did not come to fruition, the eventual destination for the premiere being Birmingham over eight years later. The next stage towards completion was Elgar's application to Chatto and Windus, publishers of O'Shaughnessy's collection of poetry entitled *Music and Moonlight*, for copyright permission to use the Ode. The matter was taken over by Alfred Littleton, Chairman of Novello Publishing, and by January 1908 copyright clearance was granted by O'Shaughnessy's literary executor, the Reverend A.W. Newport Deacon, who was delighted with the prospect of a setting by such an eminent composer. Other projects took priority over *The Music Makers*, especially the First Symphony (1908), the Violin Concerto (1910), the Second Symphony (1911) and the *Crown of India Suite* (1912), although he had been sketching ideas for his Ode in the meantime (as indicated above).

By the time Elgar came to work intensively on *The Music Makers,* he was living at Severn House (the impressive Hampstead residence to which he and Alice moved on New Year's Day 1912), and it was here that Robin Legge interviewed him on 6 January and learned that Elgar was at work on the setting of O'Shaughnessy's Ode, and had in mind as the contralto soloist Muriel Foster (1877–1937),[18] who had performed in Elgar's works several times previously,

---

[17] Martin Bird (ed.), *Edward Elgar The Path to Knighthood*: *Diaries 1902–1904*, Edward Elgar: Collected Correspondence, V/3 (Elgar Works, 2016), p. 272.

[18] *The Daily Telegraph*, 6 January 1912.

including in the Düsseldorf performance of *The Dream of Gerontius* on 19 December 1901; in the first performance of the *Coronation Ode* on 2 October 1902; in the first performance of *The Apostles* at the Birmingham Festival on 14 October 1903; and in the first performance of *The Kingdom* at the Birmingham Festival on 3 October 1906.

The move to such sumptuous, impressive surroundings as Severn House did nothing for Elgar's mood or health. On the contrary, the year was marked by debilitating ill-health. Although Elgar was often unwell, particularly with headaches, the year in question witnessed a worrying ear infection, first noted by Alice in a diary entry of 28 March,[19] and which was diagnosed as 'gout in the head', but which also manifested a visual symptom in August—namely a swollen finger.[20] Various treatments were prescribed, including taking the waters and baths. On 1 April, Elgar was obliged to follow doctor's orders of the most frustrating kind: complete rest for the whole of the month, what Elgar described, according to Alice, as 'cold storage'.[21] He was only allowed a gradual return to work in May. Despite the medical diagnosis, it is

---

[19] Alice Elgar's diary entry of 28 March 1912. The diaries of this year were transcribed by Martin Bird, who sadly died before the project reached publication. I am grateful to John Norris for providing an electronic copy of Mr Bird's transcriptions of the diaries for the years 1911, 1912, and 1913, together with a note of clarification written by Carice Elgar Blake (probably in the 1950s).

[20] Alice Elgar's diary entries of 28–30 March, and 8 August 1912.

[21] Alice Elgar's diary entries for 4 April and 24 May 1912.

possible that one cause of Elgar's illnesses was the fabric of the house itself.[22]

The settling-in period was hardly conducive to work, and Elgar's mood was not helped by trouble with the heating system, a leak resulting from nail penetration of the water pipes, and a noisy four-week period (29 May-25 June) during which his new bookshelves (designed by Arthur Troyte Griffith, his architect friend who had been given a variation in the '*Enigma*' *Variations*) were constructed.

In other words, although Elgar was often ill, the illnesses of 1912 were especially troubling and contributed to his mood of unhappiness. Other factors accounting for his sadness were the sinking of the Titanic on 8 April that year, in response to which Elgar conducted his '*Enigma*' *Variations* at a concert on 24 May for the benefit of family members of the musicians who had perished.[23]References to the '*Enigma*' *Variations* figure especially prominently in *The Music Makers*, as mentioned above, and the deeply moving reference to

---

[22] Paul Grafton, Elgar's great nephew, was kind enough to suggest a direct cause for some of Elgar's health problems: 'They had moved to Severn House in London shortly before he started work on *The Music Makers*, and he had immediately started with a mysterious illness which desperately sapped his energy, and which continued intermittently throughout the war years. We have a theory that there was some physical problem at Severn House, a little like the arsenic-impregnated wallpaper which did for Napoleon, because Edward always felt better when away from London (one of the main factors in their later taking the cottage at Brinkwells).' Email communication, 8 August 2022.

[23] Alice Elgar's diary entries for 15 April and 24 May 1912.

'Nimrod' in the Ode must have brought back memories of his departed, intimate friend and with it, further melancholy.

Elgar was unable to give the Ode his undivided attention until work on *The Crown of India* was completed. Commissioned by the Coliseum in London to celebrate the Indian Coronation of King George V and Queen Mary, the Masque was performed between 11 and 23 March, with Elgar conducting one or two performances a day (except Sundays). There were also numerous other conducting appointments to fulfil, including at Cambridge (on 1 February), Leeds (12 February), Bournemouth (9 March), London (24 May—the Titanic benefit concert mentioned above), Harrogate (28 August), and Hereford (12 September).[24]

Perhaps because of these illnesses and his mental state— including, no doubt, exhaustion after his exertions with the Masque and his busy conducting schedule—Elgar struggled with the composition of *The Music Makers*, and by 23 May (according to Alice's diary) was still 'not very happy over his work'—not 'lit up'. Hoping to find material in the 'shed music'—i.e. the wind quintets he had written during the 1870s for performance in the building behind the Elgar music shop in Worcester—he wrote to his old friend (and flautist in that quintet), Hubert Leicester on 29 May asking for loan of the scores. However, sufficient progress had been made by 18 June for Elgar to send the first section of music (up to the end of stanza 1) to Novello's for printing, by which time he was feeling much better about the composition, and on 23 June he played over passages on the piano to Harold Brooke, the chief

---

[24] Alice Elgar's diary entries for 1 and 12 February, 9 March, 23 and 24 May, 28 August, 12 September 1912.

editor and reader at Novello's. On 25 June, Muriel Foster sang over some of the solo part with Elgar, and, according to Alice, 'sang gloriously', and attended other rehearsals with Elgar on 2 and 16 July. The penultimate bundle of manuscript was delivered to Novello's on 12 July.[25]

The vocal score was completed on 18 July.[26] As mentioned above, the manuscript front cover reveals the uncertainty Elgar felt about the precise title of his composition—Ode, Symphony, or *The Music Makers*—even by this late stage. Written by Elgar (in black ink), the description reads:

To my friend/Nicholas Kilburn/Doctor of Music [crossed out]/The Music Makers/Ode [added later]/by Arthur O'Shaughnessy/Set to music/for Chorus [deleted] Contralto Solo Chorus [added above and positioned with a caret] and/orchestra/by/Edward Elgar/Op. 69/[The following description is crossed out in its entirety:] Symphony/for solo, chorus and orchestra/The Music Makers/An Ode/by/Elgar.[27]

---

[25] Alice Elgar's diary entries for 18, 23 and 25 June, 12 and 16 July 1912.

[26] Alice Elgar's diary entry for 18 July 1912.

[27] London, British Library, Add. MS. 58,036. Regarding the deletion of Nicholas Kilburn's 'Doctor of Music' title, Elgar had sought Kilburn's wishes in this respect in a letter of 5 July 1912 (with grateful thanks to Richard Westwood-Brookes for providing a copy of this letter). For further discussion of what Elgar might have thought about the symphonic aspects of the work, see Chapter 4.

Elgar's final choice of 'Ode' to describe the work places *The Music Makers* in the context of the choral ode, a subgenre heard at British Music Festivals—not as often as oratorios and cantatas, but with a catalogue of works many of which would have been known to Elgar, including Hubert Parry's *Blest Pair of Sirens* (Milton), 1887, *Ode on St Cecilia's Day* (Pope), 1889, *Ode to Music* (Benson), 1901, and Charles Villiers Stanford's *Elegiac Ode* (Walt Whitman), 1884.

As suggested by Julian Rushton, Elgar's decision to dedicate the work to Nicholas Kilburn (1843–1923), a gifted choral conductor based in Bishop Auckland and an early supporter and promoter of Elgar's music in the north east, was perhaps in compensation for the removal of his planned variation from the '*Enigma*' *Variations*—possibly because of irritation (later regretted) with Kilburn's failure (in a letter of 20 November 1898) to offer unreserved praise for Elgar's cantata, *Caractacus*.[28] According to a letter from Mrs Kilburn to Elgar, Nicholas regarded the dedication as the greatest honour of his life.[29] Correspondence between Elgar and Kilburn included the question of whether to include academic distinctions in the dedication, which explains the deletion of Doctor of Music on the title page:

Heartiest thanks for yr letter—Certainly, (dedication-wise) without the academic and other externals! Just the plain

---

[28] Julian Rushton, *Elgar: 'Enigma' Variations* (Cambridge University Press, 1999), p. 10.

[29] Letter from Alice D. Kilburn to Elgar, dated 20 February 1912, quoted in Jerrold Northrop Moore, *Edward Elgar: Letters of a Lifetime* (Oxford University Press, 1990), p. 243.

X'tian and surname, as you have it, along with the heart-gladdening word 'friend'. Almost the noblest word in our language! It to me, from you, gives true and bountiful wealth.[30]

Kilburn further showed his gratitude in the most practical way possible: by conducting an early performance.[31]

With completion of a major work usually came depression for Elgar, and the pattern was not to be broken in this case. He wrote to Alice Stuart Wortley on 19 July (the day after completion of the vocal score and submission to Novello's):

Yesterday was the usual awful day which inevitably occurs when I have completed a work: it has always been so: but this time I promised myself 'a day'! —I should be crowned—it wd. be lovely weather—and I should have open air and sympathy and everything to mark the end of the work—to get away from the labour part and dream over it happily. Yes: I was to be crowned—the first time in my life— But—I sent the last page to the printer. Alice and Carice were away for the day and I wandered alone on to the heath—it was bitterly cold—I wrapped myself in a thick overcoat and sat for two minutes, tears streaming out of my cold eyes and loathed the world—came back to the house—empty and cold—how I hated having written anything: so I wandered out again and shivered and longed to destroy the work of my

---

[30] Moore, *Edward Elgar: Letters of a Lifetime*, p. 247.

[31] 21 November 1912, at the Victoria Hall, Sunderland—see Appendix 2, Early Performances of *The Music Makers*.

hands—all wasted—and this was to have been the one real
day in my artistic life—sympathy and the end of work. :

'World losers and world-foresakers for ever and ever'
How true it is.[32]

Elgar's spirits would have been lifted by the reaction of
the conductor Hans Richter, who expressed great interest in
the work when Alice Stuart Wortley, who was at Bayreuth for
the annual festival in August, showed him proofs of the vocal
score.

Work on the full score was begun in earnest on 5 August;
orchestration of the vocal sections—i.e. from rehearsal figure
10 to the end—was completed on 13 August and taken by
Edward and Alice to Novello's on that day.[33] Orchestration of
the prelude (i.e. up to one bar before figure 10) was completed
on 20 August, at Little Langley's, Steep, Hampshire (the
home of the Elgars' friend, Winifred Murray, where Edward
and Alice had been staying since 15 August).[34] This date—20
August 1912—thus signals completion of *The Music Makers.*
Alice's assistance, as usual, was invaluable. She not only
wrote out the instrumental designations from the point of the
first choral entry to the end of the work and drew the bar lines,
but also copied all the vocal parts, including word underlay,

---

[32] Letter to Alice Stuart Wortley, quoted in Jerrold Northrop Moore,
*Edward Elgar The Windflower Letters: Correspondence with Alice
Caroline Stuart Wortley and her Family* (Oxford University Press,
1989), p. 103. Elgar's depressed state was clearly intensified by the
exceptionally cold summer that year.

[33] Alice Elgar's diary entries for 5 and 13 August 1912, with
supplementary information provided (probably in the 1950s) by
Carice Elgar Blake.

[34] Alice Elgar's diary entries for 5 and 20 August 1912.

taking great care in the process, and completed her contribution on 10 August.[35] Even with Alice's assistance, to have finished the orchestration in such a short time is testimony to Elgar's clear idea about instrumentation during the composing of the vocal score; indeed, as early as 5 July, he was able to provide Kilburn with a detailed description, including advice on what economies could be made with the collection of instruments when performing the work in the north east.[36] At the end of the full score, Elgar wrote a quotation he had previously affixed to the score of the *'Enigma' Variations*: 'Bramo assai, poco spero, nulla chieggio', a misquotation from Tasso, which Elgar had translated as 'I essay much, I hope little, I ask nothing'.[37]

---

[35] Autograph manuscript score, University of Birmingham, Cadbury Research Library, EE 3/6; the orchestral prelude (pp. 1–17) is written on separate, bespoke manuscript pages measuring 46 x 33.5 cm; there are 17 staves for woodwind, brass and timps, and 11 staves for strings; the instrumental designations are printed; the verso of each page is completely blank; pp. 18–115 are written on two-sided manuscript paper (with music written on the recto only of each page), measuring 48 x 30.5 cm; there are 33 staves on each page, with a space for percussion and three staves for organ. Alice notes in her diary entry for 10 August: 'A. finished preparing the score. So pleased [underlined] to finish it in time before E. was ready for the last part'.

[36] Letter from Elgar to Kilburn, 5 July 1912—with grateful thanks to Richard Westwood-Brookes for a copy of the letter.

[37] On Elgar's use of this quotation see Brian Trowell, 'Elgar's Use of Literature', in Raymond Monk (ed.), *Edward Elgar: Music and Literature* (Aldershot: Scolar Press, 1993), pp. 182–326, esp. pp. 213–215.

On 22 August, Elgar went through the music with R.H. Wilson, the Birmingham Chorus Master (with whom Elgar had worked previously when preparing performances of *The Apostles* and *The Kingdom*). Elgar himself directed choral rehearsals on 9 and 25 September. He corrected proofs of the orchestral parts during and after the Hereford Three Choirs Festival, 7–15 September.

The first orchestral rehearsals were held in London, on 24 (wind only) and 25 September (full orchestra) at the Queen's Small Hall, and then at Birmingham on the evening of the 25th, and again at Birmingham on 27 and 28 September.[38] The world premiere was given at Birmingham Town Hall on Tuesday, 1 October 1912, as part of the Birmingham Festival (in aid of the General Hospital), with soloist Muriel Foster and the Birmingham Festival Choir and Orchestra, conducted by the composer. The complete programme was as follows:[39]

Beethoven, 'Coriolan' Overture

Bach, Brandenburg Concerto no. 3

Liszt, Piano Concerto no. 1 in E flat (soloist: Moriz Rosenthal)

Elgar, *The Music Makers* for contralto solo, chorus and orchestra (soloist: Muriel Foster, conducted by the composer)

Interval

Sibelius, Symphony no. 4 in A minor (conducted by the composer)

Purcell, Aria 'Mad Bess' (soloist: Muriel Foster)

---

[38] Alice Elgar's diary entries for 24, 25, 27 and 28 September 1912.

[39] I am grateful to Arthur Reynolds for loan of a copy of the original printed programme.

Rosenthal, 'Humoreske on Themes of Johann Strauss'
(Moriz Rosenthal, piano)

Rossini, Overture, 'William Tell'

Programme notes for *The Music Makers* were provided by
Ernest Newman.[40] Elgar's handwritten letter and typescript
notes for the assistance of Newman are extremely revealing
about the composer's intentions generally and about the
identity and placement of the musical quotations in particular.
Clearly, Elgar knew that the main feature which would be
picked up by the critics was his novel way of incorporating
'borrowings', especially from his own music but also from
several external sources, and he was keen that Newman
should not exaggerate the extent of them in relation to the
much greater part taken up by the newly composed music.
Dated 14 August 1912, Elgar's covering letter reads:

Dear Newman

*I was glad to receive your letter and to know that you were
'doing' the Ode—Enclosed I send a typewritten copy of some
notes, or rather a sort of introductory note I made: use any of
it you like—perhaps quoted wd be the best but you can decide
otherwise if my view jumps with yours.*

*As to the themes I give you a list on another sheet—the
end of p. 17 (of wh. you ask) is a reference to the vocal parts
beginning a bar after [figure] 12, not from another work.*

*You will notice that the 1ˢᵗ vocal theme 'We are the music
makers' is used (sometimes only rhythmically suggested) as a
sort of 'artist' theme as at [figures] 16 and 44 and 60 and six*

[40] Newman's programme note first appeared in *The Musical Times*,
1 September 1912, pp. 566–570.

bars before 65 and after 82. Please do not insist too much on the extent of the quotations which after all form a very small portion of the work and it is not worthwhile to emphasise the use of Rule Britannia (in tenor) or the Marsellaise [sic] on p. 11—bar 2—although you will be interested to see how they go together and the deadly sarcasm of that rush in horns and trombones in the English tune and deliberately comically in the fifth bar after [figure] 19.

I am glad you like the idea of the quotations: after all art must be the man, and all true art is to a great extent egoism and I have written several things which are still alive— Anything further I shall be delighted to tell you.[41]

The typescript notes which describe the borrowed themes and their occurrences will be discussed later (in Chapter 4, 'Reading the Music').

The Aftermath

All seemed well around the time of the premiere. Alice wrote:

To performance of Music Makers—Most splendid and impressive. Wonderful effects of Orchn. and Chorus beautiful rendering. Muriel [Foster] splendid. E. conducted magnificently. Had a great reception—Dear Kilburns there and many friends. Frank [Schuster] much impressed. Stuart Wortleys gave a supper for E. Mr and Mrs S.W., Prof. [Charles Sanford] Terry, Frank, Mr Cobb.[42]

---

[41] London, British Library, Add. MS. 47908, p. 86.

[42] Alice Elgar's diary entry for 1 October 1912.

Over the next few months, as will be described in Chapter 2, following the Birmingham premiere, *The Music Makers* was performed the length and breadth of England—Elgar himself attending the performances at Sunderland (on 21 November) and London (on 28 November)[43]—and also in New York (on 16 April 1913), activity which should have encouraged and lifted the spirits of the composer, but this does not seem to have been the case. He was depressed, exhausted, and lonely, especially when at Severn House. He seems to have been particularly upset by one or two reviews in the press, even though there were plenty of positive notices to redress the balance.[44]

These early critical reactions to *The Music Makers* are the subject of the next chapter.

---

[43] Alice Elgar's diary entries for 21 and 28 November 1912.

[44] It may be significant that no folder of congratulatory letters in connection with *The Music Makers* was kept by Carice Elgar, as she normally did for new works by her father. This could have been on Elgar's instructions, arising from his sensitivity to the one or two negative references; see Martin Bird, 'Reactions to *The Music Makers*', *The Elgar Society Journal*, 17/6 (2012), pp. 13–15, 35.

Chapter 2
Reading the Critics

Newspapers and Journals

Received wisdom is that Elgar's *The Music Makers* was reviewed unfavourably by the earliest critics, an idea given the stamp of authority by Jerrold Northrop Moore in 1987,[45] who quotes from three relatively negative newspaper reports which followed respectively the world premiere in Birmingham on 1 October 1912 and a performance in Brighton the following month. The situation is much more nuanced than we have been led to believe, however. Of the nine newspaper reviews following the Birmingham performance, five were entirely or largely positive about the work and the audience reception. *The Birmingham Gazette*'s review,[46] appearing the day after the concert, was unrestrained in its praise of Elgar's creation and the performance of it:

---

[45] Jerrold Northrop Moore, *Edward Elgar: A Creative Life* (Oxford University Press, 1987), pp. 639–640. See also Richard Westwood-Brookes, *Elgar and the Press: A life in Newsprint* (Amazon [2019]).

[46] *The Birmingham Gazette*, 2 October 1912.

'The Music Makers', conducted by the composer and superbly sung by one of the finest choirs ever heard, had the great reception it deserved. Sir Edward Elgar has derived from O'Shaughnessy's poem a real inspiration. The mood is remindful of 'Gerontius', and there are snatches of the Enigma Variations, the finest orchestral variations ever written, in any country, by anybody. There is an alto solo, and with Miss Muriel Foster once more fortunately to the fore, the composer could rely on the most satisfactory interpretation this particular planet could afford. It would be impossible to speak too highly of the work of the choir, either as to expression or technique. Few choirs could deal with a work so exacting in the expressional demand...The piece is one of the composer's best, and his best is quite good enough for the people of today...Sir Edward has added another laurel to his crown, and...the choir have further increased the reputation of the Midlands for intelligence and technical ability.

The Daily News and Leader,[47] and *The Morning Post*,[48] also of 2 October, were scarcely less positive about the music and included reports of the numerous stage recalls demanded by the audience of both Elgar and Foster, although *The Morning Post* was critical of the poem, and *The Daily Post* rather damned Elgar's creation with faint praise.[49] *The Yorkshire Post* of 2 October enthused about the 'sympathetic and deeply felt music' and Elgar's 'dreamy charm that is altogether delightful', even if, to the reviewer's ears, the

---

[47] *The Daily News and Leader*, 2 October 1912.

[48] *The Morning Post*, 2 October 1912.

[49] *The Daily Post*, 2 October 1912.

balance between soloist and choir weighed too heavily in favour of the choir.[50] The *Christian Science Monitor* (Boston, Mass.) was not only positive about the work and the audience reception but demonstrated appreciable insight into Elgar's interpretation of the Ode.[51]

However, numerical consideration in the matter of positive against negative reviews does not necessarily provide the most crucial evidence: the national standing of the newspapers is even more significant. *The Daily Telegraph*, 2 October,[52] offered the most severe assessment (probably from Robin Legge).[53] Even here, however, there are comments which are both positive, if qualified ('the music is often of exquisite beauty') and prescient ('it is not likely to supplant several of its predecessors'). Nevertheless, a review such as this, from a leading newspaper and indeed the composer's preferred choice, must have been upsetting to a composer of Elgar's extreme sensitivity:

It has already been pointed out…that the motif of O'Shaughnessy's ode, 'The Music Makers', is the idea that the music-makers and dreamers are really the creators and inspirers of men, and their deeds the true makers of history. Elgar carries the idea somewhat further, and includes all artists who feel the tremendous responsibilities of their mission to renew the world. Elgar himself has spoken of the

---

[50] *The Yorkshire Post*, 2 October 1912.

[51] *The Christian Science Monitor* (Boston, Mass.), 5 [?] October 1912.

[52] *The Daily Telegraph*, 2 October 1912.

[53] Robin Legge's obituary appeared in *The Times*, 7 April 1933.

suffering of the creative artist [in his university lectures]; the highest ecstasy of making is mixed with the consciousness of the sombre dignity, of the eternity of the artist's responsibility, and this, no doubt, makes for the sadness of the mood that pervades so much of the music that counts. But I do not feel on one hearing of 'The Music Makers' that its note is so much of sadness as of unsatisfied yearning. The composer seems to long himself to be convinced that the music makers are what the poet represents them to be; if they are, then surely here is a case for the most glorious optimism, as of the woman whose children assist in the working-out of the world's destiny. Then, again, where the poet speaks in general terms Elgar appears to look at the personal aspect of the matter. The music is often of exquisite beauty, but I feel quite sure that although the ode represents Elgar in the highest development of his creative faculty, it is not a work likely to supplant several of its predecessors in the hearts of the generality of admirers of that faculty. Its very mood is against it—the mood of yearning, alternating with a confident mood of massive power, and finally bringing a return to the prevailing lack of confidence, as if the subject were greater than the composer could translate into terms of music.

The ode was received with great warmth as was Miss Muriel Foster, who had done wonders with the solo music, but more than once the composer, who conducted, allowed his orchestra too much dynamic licence.

The review in *The Times*, of 2 October,[54] was hardly more positive, and even damned with faint praise:

---

[54] *The Times*, 2 October 1912.

...the poem calls out new and characteristic music having many points of beautiful and intricate expression. But it is all characteristic of him as we know him; it does not place his creative powers in any new light. It reveals no unexpected possibilities in him, and so offers no obscurities to the listener at a first hearing.

The most curiously ambivalent review, in an unidentified newspaper, begins by praising the music, continues by condemning the poetry, and concludes by virtually dismissing the music. Moreover, the critic's description of the Sibelius Fourth Symphony, 'breathing a faint peculiar poetry and charm', is probably the last quality one would think of, and further casts doubt on the reliability of this critic:

A new choral work from Sir Edward Elgar, strikingly sonorous, flowing warmly, expressive in style, and obviously destined to high popularity; a new symphony from Finland, breathing a faint peculiar poetry and charm; and a whole crop of fresh laurels for Sir Henry Wood as Dr Richter's successor—such are the first fruits of the Birmingham Festival which opened with impressive audiences yesterday.

'The Music Makers', Sir Edward Elgar's new choral ode, touches none of the depths of the composer's really memorable achievements excepting by the way of direct quotation. Yet it deserves, and will win popular favour and many performances because of its fluent grace and beautiful accomplished workmanship.

Sir Edward is nowadays in the completest possession of his style of technical accomplishment. He can compose those glowing Elgarian harmonies, that rich orchestral colouring, whether he has or has not a considerable motive behind, just as Bach wrote counterpoint. But the agitated voluptuous feminine nature of Elgar's style makes his merely 'occasional' work rather dozing.

Where 'The Music Makers' falls short is in the unreality of the themes. Arthur O'Shaughnessy's ode celebrates the feats of the world's poets in forging to ideals and the destinies of their fellow-men. 'We built up the world's great cities, built Nineveh with our sighing and Babel with mirth. A breath of our inspiration is the life of each generation.' This is all very flattering to that charming race of rhymers for whom the most important thing in life is their ballads to their mistresses' eyebrows. But did a single member of the chorus who sang those words, or one person in to-night's audience, really believe them? The fallacy of the poem lies, of course, in the fact that poets have nothing to do with 'teaching humanity' or with the building of empires or cities, but solely with the charming of one's finer senses and the enrichment of one's inner life. Music set to this ode could not therefore be expected to have great strength or sincerity.

Before going any further, it is worth remembering that these newspaper reviews, some of which are quite substantial, were written in most cases virtually on the night of the performance in order to appear in print the very next day and so the reactions were pretty well immediate (although critics could have attended rehearsals). Considering how full the programme was at that concert (which included a piano concerto by Liszt and the world premiere of Sibelius's Fourth Symphony), the appearance of the reviews the very next

41

morning represents a miracle of communications when we consider that this was over a hundred and ten years ago.

It is also worth remembering the political context of these newspaper reviews. Anyone turning the pages of *The Times*, *The Daily Telegraph* or any other national newspaper would, before finding the arts review pages, have had to encounter headline after headline about the Balkan crisis (from which hostilities broke out just seven days after the premiere of *The Music Makers*). Few could have predicted that these events—involving chiefly Bulgaria, Serbia, Montenegro, Greece, the Ottoman Empire, and with keen interest from Austro-Hungary, Bosnia and Germany—would herald the inexorable march to the Great European War and subsequent World War. Nevertheless, in the face of these realities of contemporary international tension, O'Shaughnessy's claim about the music makers being the instigators of earth-shattering events must have rung hollow to at least some of the critics.

One of the most extensive reviews appeared in *The Musical Times*, 1 November 1912, and this was entirely positive about the poem, the music and the performance;[55] the following extract is a flavour of the enthusiastic review:

The performance was a remarkably fine one, and revealed most if not all of the subtle and suggestive charm of the music. The probable effect of the quotations from the composer's former works was a matter of curiosity for some listeners who, previous to the performance, harboured a feeling that mayhap the tracing of the quotations and the recollections of their former association might distract attention from their present

---

[55] *The Musical Times*, November 1912, p. 724.

application. But it turned out quite otherwise, for the leitmotives are so ingeniously and naturally dovetailed into their environment as never to obtrude and they always seem to fit the situation to a nicety. The climaxes are in places tremendous. One of the most exciting is that to the words 'Trample a kingdom down', which is almost terrible in its savage intensity. A beautiful choral section ensues to the words 'We in the ages lying'...No other choral music that Elgar has written has finer penetration or expression than that set to the words 'A breath of our inspiration/Is the life of each generation'...The introduction of the 'Novissima hora est' theme at this stage [i.e. near the end] is wonderfully eloquent and searching. After this, the music glides like a fleecy cloud to its extinction; the transition from sound to silence is almost imperceptible.

Soon after the first performance the work was performed the length and breadth of the country—Brighton (13 November), Worcester (19 November), Sunderland (21 November), London (28 November), Exmouth (November), Bristol (30 November), Liverpool (18 February), Bethnal Green (January or February), London (3 March), Bishop Auckland (March)—and in New York (16 April).

Although this multitude of performances over this six month period (as detailed in Appendix 2) cannot in itself be cited as evidence of the success of the work—since the arrangements (hiring of music, booking venues and so on) would have been made well before the Birmingham premiere—it can be cited as evidence of the great interest created by the announcement of the new work (in newspapers, as well as in the detailed analysis by Earnest Newman published in *The Musical Times* of 1 September 1912).[56]

The second performance, as part of the Brighton Festival, attracted almost as much attention from the press as the premiere, partly because it was once again conducted by the composer, and again with Muriel Foster as soloist. Most of the reviews were entirely positive. *The Sunday Times* (17 November),[57] for example, had this to say:

A further hearing confirmed the first impression of its nobility of thought and style and its fine workmanship. The choir were evidently intrigued with it and under the composer's direction gave it a very impressive performance. As at Birmingham Miss Muriel Foster gave every value to the solo part.

The only negative review was as follows from an unidentified paper:

Sir Edward Elgar's Birmingham Festival novelty, 'We are the Music Makers', is not a case of the new wine tasting like the old; in fact, it is the nips he permits us of the latter that makes the latest vintage seem lacking in flavour and bouquet. The technique of the choir was severely strained, but never to breaking point. The sopranos again distinguished themselves. Much of the music is very difficult, especially some of the entries, but on the whole careful training and familiarity with the music—many of the singers seemed to

---

[56] Ernest Newman, in *The Musical Times*, 1 September 1912.

[57] *The Sunday Times*, 17 November 1912.

have no need of their books—won the day, though a little more grip and life would have been welcome.

The solo music once more fell to that famous Elgar singer Miss Muriel Foster. It is disappointing music without the composer, as he seems so often on the verge of giving us his best only to dash hope to the ground.

Subsequent performances over the next few months met with largely enthusiastic responses. Unsurprisingly the first London performance, on 28 November, aroused most interest from the newspapers. *The Morning Post,*[58] *The Times,*[59] and *The Christian Science Monitor* all reported enthusiastically on the work and performance,[60] although an unidentified newspaper was somewhat muted in its evaluation and *The Morning Post* had little of a positive nature to say about either the work or the suitability of The Royal Albert Hall as a venue for its performance. Entirely negative, although in some details perceptive, was Charles Maclean's review in the *Zeitschrift der internationalen Musikgesellschaft* (December 1912),[61] following the London performance:

His last choral work (Birmingham Festival, 1ˢᵗ October 1912) is The Music Makers, to a rather flatulent poem by Arthur O'Shaughnessy (1844–1881), the cantata-title being only a catch-word derived from the first line. The poem

[58] *The Morning Post*, 29 November 1912.

[59] *The Times*, 29 November 1912.

[60] *The Christian Science Monitor*, 29 November 1912.

[61] Charles Maclean, Review of *The Music Makers* in the *Zeitschrift der internationalen Musikgesellschaft*, December 1912.

consists of a sustained boast that poets, and not the men of action, create the world's living and practical history; though it is generally supposed that exactly the opposite happens, and that the men of action act first and the poets sing afterwards. The diction is a key to the class of thought. Thus: 'One man with a dream, at pleasure, Shall go forth and conquer a crown: And three with a new song's measure Can trample a kingdom down.' Why one and three? This is merely the verbal titillation of the Victorian minor poet. Elgar has taken the paradox of this poem very seriously indeed, in applying it to the musical art, with a preface to that effect. He has gone beyond the poet in dwelling on the 'suffering' of the creative musician 'conscious of the sombre dignity of the eternity of his responsibility'; the poet's tone being rather down to the last assertive and jubilant. He more directly interprets the poet, when he calls it the 'duty of the artist to see that this inevitable change is progress'. As springing out of these ideas, in Elgar's conception, arises a composition, which includes a long series of musical quotations in leit-motive fashion from his own previous works, with other quotations. The whole is a very strange revelation of the composer's intentions and thoughts, criticism of which will not here be attempted. The nett [sic] result at any rate as music has found favour with few. The work has been generally considered to be rather dull, if impressive and powerful in parts. It certainly indulges in quite extensive word-painting, to the detriment of the general jubilancy which is the tenor and purport of the poem. The mannerisms of short phrase-figures iterated in varying harmonic relations, are in the weakest parts here very conspicuous.

To the present writer it appears that lyricism must be the basis of choral work, which has behind it neither dramatic effect, nor the intellectuality of established instrumental forms; and that Elgar has in this sense retrograded from his earlier standards. However, the audience has the rare opportunity at the Albert Hall of forming their own conclusions on such a point from direct comparison [between Caractacus of 1898 and the present work], and the main object of these notes is to show that that opportunity occurred. The 1000-strong chorus (Sir Frederick Bridge) is impeccable, and threw on both works the lime-light of a perfect representation, though the new work is very difficult to sing.

The USA premiere of *The Music Makers* took place on 16 April 1913, at the Carnegie Hall, New York, where it was performed to enthusiastic acclaim,[62] apart from one review, which damned the work with faint praise and spoke of the 'more than a little wearisome repetition'.

In short, most newspaper reports were enthusiastic about Elgar's new creation, but there were degrees of significant negative reaction in a small number of highly influential organs, most notably *The Daily Telegraph,* and some of the readership in Germany were given at first an entirely unfavourable impression.

Books and Articles

Similarly mixed critical responses can be found in other forms of literature (books and articles) about the composer,

---

[62] *The New York Times*, 17 April 1913.

with the most negative comments about *The Music Makers* appearing in the 1930s. John F. Porte in his *Elgar and His Music: An Appreciative Study* of 1933 was decidedly *un*appreciative about the work in question:[63]

> *The Music Makers, for all its finely coloured writing, is not great among the best of Elgar's works. As an attractive personal revelation, it is still less successful. The themes from other works quoted as indications of certain moods are unhappy and awkward in being dragged from the only association which gave them spiritual life. This latter point stresses the fact that Elgar's verbal explanations of his music appear inadequate revelations of the inner workings of his thought as expressed in compositions. Musically 'The Music Makers' is beautiful, but we may still regret that one frankly external work like 'King Olaf' was not written at this point.*

A similarly negative view, but even more forcefully expressed, about the self-quotations came in 1935 in an influential article by Frank Howes:[64]

> *Elgar thought well of* The Music Makers *because he admired the poem. But being passionately excited about a poem may even preclude the imagination from getting to grips with it…[The composer appears to have] felt so strongly that*

---

[63] John F. Porte, *Elgar and His Music: An Appreciative Study* (London: Sir Isaac Pitman & Sons Ltd, 1933), pp.48–49.

[64] Frank Howes, 'The Two Elgars', in *Music and Letters*, February 1935, pp. 26–29, quoted in Christopher Redwood (ed.), *The Elgar Companion* (Ashbourne: Sequola Publishing, 1982), pp. 258–262.

the truth of the [poem] completely expressed [his] own feelings that [he] had nothing more to add...The self-quotations...were deliberately made but they are proof of a less than half-stirred imagination. A composer may take an indifferent text and so dwell with it that he digests and absorbs it and makes from it a great work, but he will in that case have created, not borrowed, music for it. The second-hand music in The Music Makers *is evidence not of simple vanity (as it might have been in* Heldenleben*) but of a weak impulse to compose it...The total effect of* The Music Makers *is of something below Elgar's best, of something with a streak of tawdriness in it.*

Against this, Thomas F. Dunhill, writing in 1938, extols the virtues of the work but, like Howes, finds the use of self-quotation less than successful:[65]

The most curious feature of the setting...is the extensive use which the composer has made of self-quotation...In no case is the actual progress of the music held up, but nevertheless the method, carried to such lengths and used so persistently, is disturbing.

One finds oneself wondering, over and over again, if any special point has been missed, and, when some particularly Elgarian turn of phrase appears, it is difficult to avoid searching for some illusion which may not really be there at all. The work, however, has many beauties...In the matter of technical mastery it is fully equal, if not superior, to the

---

[65] Thomas F. Dunhill, *Sir Edward Elgar* (London and Glasgow: Blackie, 1938), pp. 119–120.

greatest of its predecessors in the same medium...the imaginative faculty has never been more warmly alive, nor the mastery which directed its expression more abundantly evident.

In more recent times, critical opinion has continued to be divided. Jerrold Northrop Moore, who has done more than most to establish Elgar's reputation as one of Britain's greatest composers, ends his perceptive analytical description of the work with a negative conclusion:[66]

Edward set [the words 'Yet we are the movers and shakers Of the world for ever, it seems'] with another big 'Enigma' quotation. It showed the trouble that was to pursue the entire setting; the assurance he was seeking was beyond the assurance of his own art.

Moore's more recent assessment was decidedly scathing:

The result [of the self-quotations] is to render The Music Makers *fundamentally spasmodic. It shows no compelling musical logic. Through and through this setting, the long pulses and rhythms which guided Elgar's music through all his life in the country about Worcester, Malvern and Hereford are interrupted and upset...The fact was that* The Music Makers, *despite the strongest invitations in all his music, had failed to achieve any synthesis.*[67]

---

[66] Moore, *Edward Elgar: A Creative Life*, p. 633.

[67] Moore, *Elgar: Child of Dreams* (London: Faber and Faber, 2004), pp. 171–172.

In his book for the Associated Board of the Royal Schools of Music, J.P.E. Harper-Scott proposes, surprisingly, that one of the reasons for Elgar's choosing self-quotation was time pressure—although it is perhaps doubtful if such a method would actually save time.[68] A somewhat more positive view is presented by Diana McVeagh's perceptive, but not uncritical, appraisal,[69] and perhaps the most positive views come from Michael Kennedy, who described the work as 'one of Elgar's most endearing and unjustly under-rated works',[70] and two highly perceptive essays appeared in the *Elgar Journal* on the hundredth anniversary of the work's premiere.[71] The most detailed analysis, full of insightful and stimulating thoughts, is Aidan J. Thomson's essay in *Elgar Studies.*[72]

Other Considerations

Another indication of the chequered reputation of *The Music Makers* can be seen in the history of performances at The Three Choirs Festival. It was not until 1920 that the

[68] J.P.E. Harper-Scott, *Elgar: An Extraordinary Life* (London: The Associated Board of the Royal Schools of Music, 2007), p. 84.

[69] Diana McVeagh, *Elgar the Music Maker* (Woodbridge: The Boydell Press, 2007), pp. 142–147.

[70] Michael Kennedy, *Portrait of Elgar* (London, New York, Toronto: Oxford University Press, 1968), p. 212.

[71] Donald Hunt, 'Thoughts on *The Music Makers*: A Conductor's Viewpoint, *The Elgar Society Journal,* 17, 6, pp. 4–12; Martin Bird, 'Reactions to The Music Makers', The Elgar Society Journal, 17,6, pp. 13-15.

[72] Aidan J. Thomson, 'Unmaking *The Music Makers'*, *Elgar Studies*, (ed.) J.P.E. Harper-Scott and Julian Rushton (Cambridge University Press, 2007), pp. 99–134.

clerical authorities would permit the work in a cathedral, perhaps the mention of God in the penultimate verse sanctioning a performance after all.[73] Up to present, there have been only ten performances (Worcester 1920, Hereford 1927, Worcester 1932, Worcester 1938, Worcester 1975, Gloucester 1983, Hereford 1988, Gloucester 2004, Hereford 2012, Worcester 2021), with none at all during the period 1946–1974. This contrasts with 64 performances of *The Dream of Gerontius* over the same period, 24 of *The Kingdom* and 16 of *The Apostles*.

Perhaps yet another indication of the work's fluctuating status can be traced in the number of performances at the BBC Promenade concerts: heard first in 1944, *The Music Makers* was a fairly regular fixture until 1954 (1944, 1947, 1950, 1951, 1952, 1953, 1954), but was not performed again until 1993 (then in 2004, 2017 and 2019).

In short, *The Music Makers* has divided critical opinion, perhaps more than any other major Elgar work, and performances of it have been far less frequent than some other choral works, especially *Gerontius, The Apostles* and *The Kingdom*.

---

[73] See Donald Hunt, *Elgar and the Three Choirs Festival* (Worcester: Osborne, 1999), various places. A recording was conducted by Elgar as part of the Hereford Festival in 1927, with all passages involving soloist Olga Haley removed (as she was contracted to a rival recording company); HMV, D13491; thereafter no complete recording was made until 1967, with Sir Adrian Boult conducting the London Philharmonic Choir and soloist Janet Baker; see Jerrold Northrop Moore, *Elgar on Record: The Composer and the Gramophone* (Oxford University Press, 1974), pp. 73 ff.

The two most recurring criticisms have been of the poem and of Elgar's method of self-quotation, both aspects of which will be examined, beginning in the next chapter with the poetry.

Chapter 3
Reading the Poetry

'Ode' by the English poet Arthur O'Shaughnessy (1844–1881) is from a collection of 34 poems entitled *Music and Moonlight*, published in 1874. Beginning with the line 'We are the music makers', the Ode is the best (and in most cases only) known poem by O'Shaughnessy. That his poetry *as a whole* deserves to be better known and his place in the literary canon reappraised are persuasively argued in a recent, authoritative study by Jordan Kistler.[74]

O'Shaughnessy's poems are gathered in the following collections:[75]

---

[74] Jordan Kistler, *Arthur O'Shaughnessy, A Pre-Raphaelite Poet in the British Museum* (London and New York: Routledge, 2016). Other studies are: Louise Chandler Moulton, *Arthur O'Shaughnessy: His Life and Work with Selections from his Poems* (London: Elkin Matthews and John Lane, 1894), and Molly Whittington-Egan, *Arthur O'Shaughnessy: Music Maker* (Liverpool: The Bluecoat Press, 2013).
[75] Arthur O'Shaughnessy, *An Epic of Women and Other Poems,* (London: John Camden Hotten, 1870); *Lays of France (Founded on the Lays of Marie)*, 2nd edition (London: Chatto and Windus, 1874); *Music and Moonlight: Poems and Songs* (London: Chatto and

An Epic of Women and other Poems, 1870: 12 poems plus 'An Epic of Women' (26 poems).

Lays of France (Founded on the Lays of Marie), 1872: 4 poems.

Music and Moonlight: Poems and Songs, 1874.

Songs of a Worker, published posthumously, 1881: 23 poems plus 'Thoughts in Marble' (12 poems), 'Colibri' (3 cantos), 'Translations from Contemporary Poets' (Léon Dierx, François Coppée, André Lemoyne, Paul Verlaine, Ernest d'Hervilly, Sully Prudhomme, Henri Cazalis, Catulle Mendès, 27 poems).

According to Kistler, distinctive influences on O'Shaughnessy's poetry can be discerned in the French poetry of Victor Hugo, Charles Baudelaire and Théophile Gautier, which in turn influenced the English poetic movements of Aestheticism and Decadence, especially in the works of Algernon Charles Swinburne and Walter Pater. O'Shaughnessy was a gifted linguist and acquired native fluency in both the spoken and written forms of French. During his frequent visits to Paris, he met Victor Hugo, one of O'Shaughnessy's poetic heroes. His Francophile leanings can be appreciated especially in his *Lays of France.*[76]

Windus, 1874)*; Songs of a Worker* (London: Chatto and Windus, 1881).

[76] From the abundance of examples, perhaps the following will serve (from 'The Lay of Eliduc'), where the words of Eliduc doubtless echo O'Shaughnessy's own feelings for France:

Hard is the banishment from thee,

Fair France! And, like a minstrelsy,

The very naming of thy lands

Notably revealed in the *Lays of France* is another strand: 'Medievalism', an aspect strengthened by O'Shaughnessy's links with the Pre-Raphaelite circle of Dante Gabriel Rossetti, Swinburne and William Morris, and later followers such as Ford Madox Brown and John Payne.

In his last collection, *Songs of a Worker,* O'Shaughnessy expresses notions of 'Art for humanity', after his idol Victor Hugo,[77] and also, perhaps, under the influence of Morris and his Arts and Crafts ideal. (O'Shaughnessy's most eloquent expression of the union of artist and worker is perhaps the 'Song of a Fellow Worker'.[78])

In the poetry of O'Shaughnessy, this mixing of French, medieval, and socialist ingredients, with the seasoning of aestheticism, produced a heady, characteristic flavour. Contrasts abound: the poet is of the people and yet must remain apart; optimism is nearly always tinged with sadness. Above all, the artwork lives on after the artist is with us no more.

For many, the most captivating aspects of O'Shaughnessy's poetry may well be their relationship to music in the rhymes and rhythms, accents and syncopations. To invoke Walter Pater's 'All art constantly aspires to the condition of music' perhaps raises more questions than it answers, but the

---

Rouseth the heart, and eke the hands

Of any son indeed of thine,

In any land of the sunshine

[77] See the preface to *Songs of a Worker.*

[78] I carve the marble of pure thought until the thought takes form,
Until it gleams before my soul and makes the world grow warm;
Until there comes the glorious voice and words that seem divine,
And the music reaches all men's hearts and draws them into mine.

inherently *musical* elements of the poetry are undeniable.[79] Often, the poet sets up a metrical scheme and then breaks it, thereby confounding expectation in the manner of countless musical masterpieces, especially of the eighteenth and nineteen centuries. Other devices, such as stresses moving against the prevailing metre, are analogous to syncopation. Dramatic changes of metre are equivalent to changes of tempo or time signature or both. Changes of image or topic are equivalent to changes of key, mode or dynamic. Such aspects can, of course, be found in much, even most, fine poetry but are likely to be a primary feature, at least to some readers, of O'Shaughnessy—and his love of music (especially of Chopin) and reported expertise as a pianist can hardly have been insignificant factors.[80] These elements, along with the manifesto of music's importance, which runs through the poetry, especially in the 'Ode', as well as the idea of the

---

[79] Walter Pater, *The Renaissance: Studies in Art and Poetry*, revised edition (London and New York: Macmillan, 1888), p. 140.

[80] Occasional reference is made to Chopin, as, for example, in the following lines:

Then, unto her, enchanted in that dim
Enchanted chamber, lured by the delight
Of some arpeggio's murmur, or the slight
Immortal fantasy of some frail rhythm,
There came the lovely spirit even of him
Whom all her soul loved—Chopin, magical,
Seraphic, enigmatic, deathless—yea,
And took her on strange voyaging far away
In a sweet silver bark o'er mystical
Melodious waves beneath the moon's strange ray.
'Music and Moonlight' (from *Music and Moonlight*).

loneliness of the artist and so on, must have been what drew Elgar to the verses in the first place.

If we now focus on the Ode in question, the first poem in the collection *Music and Moonlight,* we find these characteristics from the outset:

> We are the music makers,
> And we are the dreamers of dreams,
> Wandering by lone sea-breakers,
> And sitting by desolate streams;-
> World-losers and world-forsakers,
> On whom the pale moon gleams:
> Yet we are the movers and shakers
> Of the world for ever, it seems.

Here in this opening verse we have some of the contrasts discussed above between lonely artists and what they can achieve, an image (as discussed in Chapter 2) which so irritated some critics following the first performance of Elgar's setting in 1912, and which so coloured their appraisal of the music: artists who can move and shake the world (which is announced unexpectedly and dramatically at the end of this stanza), rather than move and shake only the emotions. However, O'Shaughnessy is dealing in poetic conceit rather than literal meaning, and the image is surely to be taken metaphorically.

As mentioned above, the appeal to Elgar of O'Shaughnessy's poetic conceit would have been immediate. So often, he recalled sitting alone by the reed beds of the

Severn and hearing 'music in the air'.[81] And so often before success with the '*Enigma*' *Variations*, Elgar felt himself to be a 'loser', not in the sense of this verse but in his inability to establish himself as a composer; the lines would surely have brought back unhappy memories of his and Alice's first return from London to the West Midlands (1891) after his failures in the capital. In short, this sense of failure was a recurring theme in letters during periodic dark moods throughout his life.[82]

O'Shaughnessy uses two rhyming schemes for this poem: ABABABAB (for stanzas 1, 3, 7, 8, 9) and AABBCDCD (for stanzas 2, 4, 5, 6). The first scheme is unified to a degree by metre, typically dactyl, spondee, spondee for the first line, and dactyl, dactyl, spondee for the second line, providing a gentle pace. (In the examples below, the italics indicate rhythmic stress and the slashes rhythmic silence to complete the metric feet.)

We are the *mu*sic *ma*kers,

And *we* are the *drea*mers of *dreams*,

The second scheme begins more urgently, with a tendency to punch out its metre in the first two lines. Thus, we are introduced to the two varieties in alternation, followed by a sequence of the second, more urgent scheme, continuing with alternations, and ending with the opening one. This large-

---

[81] Robert J. Buckley, *Sir Edward Elgar* (London: John Lane: The Bodley Head, 1905), p. 32; letter to Sir Sidney Colvin, 13 December 1921, cited in Jerrold Northrop Moore, *Edward Elgar: A Creative Life* (Oxford University Press, 1987), p. 32.

[82] It will be recalled—see Chapter 1—that Elgar quotes bitterly from stanza 1, line 5, during an especially dark mood when writing to Alice Stuart Wortley on 19 July 1912, the day after completing the vocal score of *The Music Makers*.

scale symmetry results in a satisfying poetic experience,[83] and provided Elgar with ideal contrasts for his musical structure. Stanza two offers the most vivid contrast of image and, for those with an ear to appreciate such matters, rhythm and metre.

> With wonderful deathless ditties
> We build up the world's great cities,
> And out of a fabulous story
> We fashion an empire's glory:
> One man with a dream, at pleasure,
> Shall go forth and conquer a crown;
> And three with a new song's measure
> Can trample a kingdom down.

Here, the imagery is about what the artist can achieve. It was problematic for some of the critics in 1912 and is likely to be problematic, for different reasons, for some readers today. In 1912, an inappropriate literal reading resulted in protests from some about the absurdity of the claims for what the music makers can achieve (as discussed in Chapter 2). For today's audience, the issue is likely to be about the supposed glorification of Empire building, the subjugation of peoples (and the inevitable historical links with slavery).

---

[83] The admittedly vague word 'satisfying' is used here in the sense of intellectual ease resulting from readily identifiable structures. This very factor may, of course, be *un*satisfying, even irritating, to some readers and listeners. Grateful thanks are due to Jordan Kistler (email correspondence) for querying the use of this word in this context.

O'Shaughnessy, however, as an inhabitant of the centre of the British Empire, was using approved, metaphorical imagery of the day—together with a 'Praterian' triumph of emotional effect over literal meaning—rather than anticipating the sensibilities of a later age.[84] There may also be a problem for modern readers with some of the rhyming couplets, especially 'ditties' and 'cities', and their seemingly crude manufacture, but there is no evidence that the reading public of O'Shaughnessy's day (especially those with knowledge of Chaucer or Shakespeare) would have been troubled. In any case, the word 'ditties' is perhaps meant to conjure up an image from the medieval world in the manner of the Pre-Raphaelites.

Whatever misgivings then or now, there is no doubt about the chief strength of the poem to this point: contrasts of rhythm and metre; notice the abrupt shift at stanza 2 with its startling energy. In musical terms, we would speak of anacruses (on the unaccented syllables) followed by crashing downbeats (on the accented syllables) ending with syncopation:

With *won*derful *death*less *dit*ties—/

We *build* up the *world's* great *cit*ies—/

The internal rhythms are also noteworthy: a similar metric scheme for the AA lines, changing for the BB lines:

And out of a fabulous *sto*ry

We fashion an empire's *glo*ry:

---

[84] However, as pointed out by Dr Kistler (email correspondence), there are some 'uncomfortable poems which enact fantasies of empire that perhaps go beyond even the standard of the day (…particularly… "Colibri" and "Black Marble")'.

and changing again for the CDCD lines (where the easing of energy in the first line is answered by renewed energy in the second):

One man with a *dream*, at pleasure,/

Shall go *forth* and conquer a *crown*;/

As the momentum leads to the climax of the final line of this stanza and the strongest accent yet on the word 'trample'.

And *three* with a new song's *mea*sure/

Can *tram*ple a kingdom down./

A poet needs a high degree of rhythmic sensibility to achieve such contrasts, and once again we must refer to O'Shaughnessy's serious interest in music, especially Chopin. The Ode's rhythmic virtuosity must be another reason why Elgar was so drawn to it. Anyone already familiar with the music will hear the *con fuoco* energy of Elgar's setting of stanza 2 without a note being sounded.

In stanza 3, O'Shaughnessy's metaphorical conceit of what the music makers are capable turns to the ancient cities of Nineveh and Babel:

We, in the ages lying
In the buried past of the earth,
Built Nineveh with our sighing,
And Babel itself in our mirth;
And o'erthrew them with prophesying
To the old of the new world's worth;
For each age is a dream that is dying,
Or one that is coming to birth.

The theme of continuity is here made clear: the contrast between death is followed by birth, birth by death.

There is another point about this verse, which must have been of significance to Elgar: the evoking of Babel and the unspoken reference to Nimrod, the ruler who, according to post-biblical legend, commissioned the Tower of Babel. Elgar's Nimrod, August Jaeger, is destined to feature later in the Ode, just as he did in an earlier masterpiece by Elgar.

In stanza 4, the words 'breath', 'inspiration', 'dreaming', 'dream' are perhaps redolent of the aesthetics of Swinburne and Pater, whilst the image of 'the soldier, the king and the peasant' in the same breath as 'are working together as one', may transport us to the socialism of William Morris, where equal value can be placed on individuals of different rank, who all play their part in the creative movement.

A breath of our inspiration
Is the life of each generation;
A wondrous thing of our dreaming
Unearthly, impossible seeming—
The soldier, the king, and the peasant
Are working together in one,
Till our dream shall become their present,
And their work in the world be done.

Such imagery, such vivid contrast between the gentle and the military, the dreamlike and the practical, could only be a godsend to a composer of Elgar's sensibility.

Stanza 5 moves from the first-person plural ('we') voices of the earlier verses to the third person plural ('they') and then to the third person singular ('he'): in other words, from the collective to the individual:

> They had no vision amazing
> Of the goodly house they are raising;[85]
> They had no divine foreshowing
> Of the land to which they are going:
> But on one man's soul it hath broken,
> A light that doth not depart;
> And his look, or a word he hath spoken,
> Wrought flame in another man's heart.

Such a change is striking and introduces a highly personal element. Did O'Shaughnessy have in mind one of his poetic heroes, such as Victor Hugo, Swinburne, or Pater?[86] As will be discussed in the next chapter, Elgar seized the opportunity of this switch to the intimate to portray, in a manner both

---

[85] Benedict Taylor points to the influence of Immanuel Kant in these lines; see Taylor, *The Melody of Time: Music and Temporality in the Romantic Era* (Oxford University Press, 2016), pp. 257–289.

[86] To promote in this context the candidature of John Payne—the dedicatee of O'Shaughnessy's first volume of poetry, *An Epic of Women, and Other Poems* (1870), and who reciprocated with his own volume of the same year, *The Masques of Shadows and Other Poems*—is tempting but would be wrong, for by this stage, O'Shaughnessy and Payne had fallen out over their rivalry for the affections of one Helen Snee; see Kistler, *Arthur O'Shaughnessy*, pp. 162–163.

unambiguous and deeply moving, the one who had been his closest male friend and confidant, August Jaeger.

Stanza 6 returns to the high energy of stanza 2, with conceits about the present and the past, the acceptance of a faith previously rejected, dreams of a new generation against the rejected dreams of the old:

And therefore to-day is thrilling
With a past day's late fulfilling;
And the multitudes are enlisted
In the faith that their fathers resisted
And, scorning the dream of to-morrow,
Are bringing to pass, as they may,
In the world, for its joy or its sorrow,
The dream that was scorned yesterday.

Stanza 7 sees a return to the mood, metre, rhyming scheme and rhythms of the opening stanza: dreaming, sorrowful music makers who must remain a little apart from the rest of humanity despite their superior foresight of the 'glorious futures':

But we, with our dreaming and singing,
Ceaseless and sorrowless we!
The glory about us clinging
Of the glorious futures we see,
Our souls with high music ringing:
O men! It must ever be
That we dwell, in our dreaming and singing,
A little apart from ye.

The possibilities presented here by the imagery of 'high music ringing', and 'dreaming and singing' for a composer of the sensibility and brilliance of Elgar hardly need further comment.

Stanza 8 builds to a climax with a series of prefaces before the release of 'Once more God's future draws nigh', which is the first mention of the Almighty, although there have been biblical references, especially in stanza 3. Like a musical *decrescendo* after a grand climax, the text dies down with the warning of death for those of the past. Once again, for a composer of the magnitude of Elgar, the direction of the music for his setting is almost dictated by the text.

> For we are afar with the dawning
> And the suns that are not yet high,
> And out of the infinite morning
> Intrepid you hear us cry—
> How, spite of your human scorning,
> Once more God's future draws nigh,
> And already goes forth the warning
> That ye of the past must die.

A rhetorical cry opens the final stanza. After the massive imagery of the opening and the brilliant imagery following, the voices soften and the pace slackens as the lonely singer is silenced forever. The mood is not despondent for we have already been assured of the emergence of a new generation of singers from 'the dazzling unknown shore'.[87]

---

[87] Perhaps Elgar remembered lines 1–6 as he prepared his inaugural lectures for delivery as the Peyton Professor of Music at the

Great hail! we cry to the comers
From the dazzling unknown shore;
Bring us hither your sun and your summers,
And renew our world as of yore;
You shall teach us your song's new numbers,
And things that we dreamed not before:
Yea, in spite of a dreamer who slumbers,
And a singer who sings no more.

As we will see in the next chapter, Elgar avoids the obvious in his setting of this stanza, and perhaps by taking a leaf out of Beethoven's book, builds up a magnificent textual as well as textural, climax. As we will further see in the next chapter, the composer's interpretation of the final stanza takes a different turn from the poet's meaning.

University of Birmingham (March 1905–November 1906), during which he declared that only his faith in the younger generation of composers (among others, Havergal Brian, Vaughan Williams?) assuaged his despondency about the sterile, imitative style of 'English' music over the past 25 years (though he tactfully avoids naming names in his despondency, and even more tactfully excepts Hubert Parry from his strictures, he must have had in mind Charles Villiers Stanford, Alexander Mackenzie, and possibly the late Arthur Sullivan). See Percy M. Young (ed.), *A Future for English Music and other Lectures by Edward Elgar: Peyton Professor of Music in the University of Birmingham* (London: Dennis Dobson, 1968), especially pp. 37–55.

Elgar, the Pre-Raphaelites and O'Shaughnessy

Elgar was drawn to the Pre-Raphaelites and may, at certain times, have identified with them and members of the later Aesthetics movement to a degree.[88] He greatly admired John Everett Millais, father of his muse Alice Stuart Wortley (the Windflower), especially his painting 'Isabella'; he wrote to the Windflower after another viewing of this painting in March 1914, exclaiming, '…bless you for having such a father and bless him for having such a daughter!'[89] He admired the paintings and poetry of Rossetti, whose translation from Cavalcanti he set as 'Go, song of mine', and he quoted from William Morris in the full score of *The Apostles*. Elgar was probably drawn to O'Shaughnessy not only because of the Ode but because the circumstances of the poet's life mirrored in certain fundamental respects his own. Indeed, there were interesting parallels between the lives and aspirations of the poet and the composer, to such an extent as to make them, to a degree, kindred spirits.

Arthur O'Shaughnessy was cast into a world of straightened circumstances when his father died in 1861, leaving his mother to raise two children in the home of her elder sister. Despite these difficulties, Arthur received a good education and, as already described, became fluent in French

---

[88] Geoffrey Hodgkins, 'E's Favourite Picture: Elgar and the Pre-Raphaelites', *The Victorian Webb: Literature, History and Culture in the Age of Victoria* (2007),
https://victorianweb.org/mt/elgar/1.htm.

[89] Jerrold Northrop Moore, *Edward Elgar The Windflower Letters: Correspondence with Alice Caroline Stuart Wortley* (Oxford University Press), p. 131.

and possessed a distinct gift for music. Unable to attend university because of lack of funds, at the age of seventeen (thanks to the good offices of Edward Bulwer-Lytton, whose novel, *A Strange Story*, was incidentally destined to stir the imagination of Elgar many years later at Brinkwells), he obtained a position at the British Museum, where he worked for the rest of his short life, firstly as a transcriber in the Department of Printed Books, and three years later as a cataloguer of fish and reptiles. The day-job from this point required him to exist 'in his queer little subterranean cell, strongly scented with spirits of wine, and with grim creatures pickled round him in rows on rows of gallipots'. Edmund Gosse's description may strike us as both humorous and evocative but probably falls not far short of O'Shaughnessy's own depressed attitude to his job,[90] for he clearly lacked interest, aptitude and application, as evidenced by the reprimands and negative reports issued by his superiors.[91] In short, as further observed by Gosse, 'his heart was never in his gallipots. His heart was on his sleeve, and the only matters which really interested him were verse and the passion of love, after which he thirsted as harts do after water-brooks'[92]

In other words, his passion for poetry was as great as his antagonism towards his salaried position. And here was the rub, for O'Shaughnessy saw himself as a poet, and resented

---

[90] Edmund Gosse, 'Obituary: Arthur O'Shaughnessy', in *The Academy*, 457 (5 February 1881), pp. 98–99. See also Moulton, *Arthur O'Shaughnessy*, pp. 14–15.

[91] As documented by Kistler, *Arthur O'Shaughnessy*, pp. 28–34.

[92] Edmund Gosse, *Silhouettes* (London: Heinemann, 1925), p. 175. *Silhouettes* is a selection of Gosse's writings for *The Sunday Times*.

having to work in another job to survive, leaving time for poetry only in his leisure hours. In this respect, he contrasted his circumstances to the English poets he most admired—Swinburne, Pater, Rossetti, Morris—all of whom benefited from material and educational advantages which permitted devotion to their art without the depressing need to earn a living, and in whose circle he was confined to the periphery. In other words, his short life may well have been coloured by feelings of envy and inferiority.

Elgar was similarly afflicted. Born 'into trade'—the son of a piano tuner and music shop proprietor in the West Midlands—he was ever conscious of his inferior circumstances, a realisation made acute by the strict class system of his age. Even with the honours heaped on him—a knighthood, KCVO, GCVO, Baronetcy, OM, Master of the King's Music—the feeling of inferiority against his socially and educationally advantaged contemporaries, Stanford and Parry, persisted. An article in the *Handbuch der Musik Geschichte* (1930) by the distinguished music professor E.J. Dent compared Elgar unfavourably with those two composers, against whom Elgar, according to Dent, 'possessed little of the literary culture';[93] not only was this assessment unfair, it was also the cruellest confirmation of Elgar's lifelong, fearful instinct about the immutability of his social status.

At times in his career, Elgar was compelled to undertake work in which he had no interest and of which he was ashamed, in a similar way to O'Shaughnessy's attitude to his work at the British Museum. Violin teaching was especially

---

[93] Moore, *Edward Elgar: A Creative Life,* pp. 789–790.

irksome for Elgar, both the activity and the status. Following marriage to the high-born Alice Roberts in 1889, Elgar tried to establish his reputation in London as a composer, but without success, and even the desperate fall-back position of seeking to establish a practice as a violin teacher failed. The reluctant return to Worcestershire in June 1891 and the dreaded and despised trade (from his point of view) of the itinerant violin teacher in the provinces were heavy blows to his self-esteem.[94]

Their avocations were also related, though in opposite directions. O'Shaughnessy's primary passion was for poetry with, as discussed, a secondary but deep interest in music. Musical references abound in his poems; 'Music and Moonlight', 'A Love Symphony' and 'A Duet: Piano and Violoncello' (from *Songs of a Worker*); 'A Neglected Harp' (*An Epic of Women and Other Poems*), 'Song of a Fellow Worker' (*Songs of a Worker*), 'Charmed Moments (Chopin's Nocturne, Op. 37, No. 1)' (*An Epic of Women*), and many more, and the references to song and singing are similarly innumerable. Elgar's passion for literature—especially Shakespeare, Swinburne,[95] Morris, Longfellow, and French,

---

[94] For an account of Elgar's apparently resentful attitude to violin teaching, see Rosa Burley and Frank Carruthers, *Edward Elgar: The Record of a Friendship* (London: Barrie and Jenkins, 1972), pp. 18–21. Also significant is Robert Buckley's report of Elgar's likening teaching in general to 'turning a grindstone with a dislocated shoulder'; Buckley, *Sir Edward Elgar,* p. 43. For a more positive witness account of Elgar's teaching, however, see Moore, *Edward Elgar: A Creative Life*, p. 172.

[95] As noted by Brian Trowell in his virtuoso article, 'Elgar's Use of Literature', in Raymond Monk (ed.), *Edward Elgar: Music and*

Italian and German literature in translation (especially Victor Hugo, Tasso and Goethe)—was second only to his devotion to music.

Although O'Shaughnessy was a reluctant scientist, this was to remain his primary occupation—and he did eventually achieve a degree of recognition as a herpetologist and ichthyologist as evidenced by a small number of publications from 1869, 1874 and 1875. For Elgar, science, and especially chemistry, stood as a serious interest for much of his life. Experiments in his garden-laboratory, The Ark, even led to a patented scientific instrument, the 'Sulphuretted Hydrogen Apparatus', in 1908.

In short, both O'Shaughnessy and Elgar were extremely sensitive about being 'outsiders', about their class, their circumstances, especially their lack of private incomes; Elgar's sensibility was further heightened by his faith as a Catholic in a Protestant country. Nevertheless, both (especially Elgar) achieved recognition, against what often appeared to be insuperable obstacles, in their respective creative endeavours.

We do not know the extent to which these similarities of circumstance and psychology were of conscious significance

---

Literature (Aldershot: Scolar Press, 1993), pp. 182–326, see especially p. 191, Elgar copied, at some unspecified time, the first four lines of Swinburne's 'A Leave-Taking':
Let us go hence, my songs, she will not hear:
Let us go hence together without fear;
Keep silence now, for singing-time is over:
And over all old things and all things dear.

to Elgar,[96] but life experiences undoubtedly informed the

---

[96] Elgar acquired at least some of his information about the circumstances of O'Shaughnessy's life from his copy of the *Encyclopaedia Britannica,* 10th edition (Edinburgh and London: Adam and Charles Black; London: The Times, 1902), which he acquired in December 1902. The substantial entry on 'O'Shaughnessy, Arthur William Edgar (1844–1881)', includes details of his position in the natural history department of the British Museum, for which 'he had probably little natural aptitude, but he so carefully qualified himself as to become in time an authority.' The collections of poetry are listed, with the following assessment of his assumed strengths and weaknesses (which assessments must have been sanctioned by Edmund Gosse, editor of the literature entries and author of O'Shaughnessy's obituary in *The Academy* (1881), and whom Elgar met in 1910): 'The qualities of O'Shaughnessy's poetry are those of the true singer; the defect the lack of importance in theme and dignity in thought. His melodies are often magnificent; and, as in *The Fountain of Tears*, the richness of his imagery conceals a certain vagueness and indecision of the creative faculty. He was also very felicitous in bold uses of repetition and echo, by which he secured effects which for haunting melody are almost inimitable. His spirit is that of a mild melancholy, drifting helplessly through the realities of life and spending itself in song. Where the inspiration of that moment fails him, and nothing but the music is left, the insubstantiality of his talent becomes clear. By some critics, he has been occasionally disparaged, but reparation was done to his memory by Francis Turner Palgrave, who, in the second series of the *Golden Treasury*, said with some exaggeration that his metrical gift was the finest, after Tennyson, of any of the later poets, and that he had "a haunting music all his own."' For sure, these emphases on the musical qualities of the poetry were probably enough to attract Elgar on their own. A handwritten copy of this entry was made by Alice Elgar (London, British Library,

creative processes of the two in ways which were not entirely dissimilar, and it would be surprising if such a questioning intelligence as Elgar's was not acutely aware of this. As observed by his contemporaries, O'Shaughnessy strove to imbue his poetry with musical qualities. In *The Music Makers* the union between verse and music is realised to the highest degree.

Add. MS. 47908, ff.102–104). The account by Louise Chandler Moulton (who had met O'Shaughnessy), *Arthur O'Shaughnessy*, contains an elegant tribute to the poet—although her assessment of his strengths and weaknesses is equally open to disagreement—and could well have been known to Elgar.

Chapter 4
Reading the Music

Musical Quotations

The most famous aspect of Elgar's *The Music Makers*—the quotations, especially self-quotations—has already been touched on in chapters one and two but demands greater attention here. In his NOTE, which he wrote to assist Ernest Newman who was writing the programme note for the first performance, Elgar explained as follows:

Coming to the actual musical setting, there are one or two particulars which may be noted. Throughout the work, some quotations appear: two of these are snatches of national airs, the others are from my own compositions. It is scarcely necessary to specify these in detail: if the original place of any of these themes is known to the hearer, he may feel the reason for its presence, and perhaps, appreciate the propriety and appositeness of its inclusion here. If these quoted passages are unknown, the music may be listened to simply as an expression of feelings called up by the poem, without regard to the quotations as such.

I have used the opening bars of the theme 'Enigma' of the

Variations because it expressed when written (in 1898) my sense of the loneliness of the artist as described in the first six lines of the Ode, to me, and it still embodies that sense; at the end of the score of the Variations I wrote, 'Bramo assai, poco spero, nulla chieggio' (Tasso).[97]

Occasionally, I have departed from a general interpretation of the words, as an orator leaves the broad view of his subject to give a particular instance; at 'We are the dreamers of dreams', the theme quoted refers to a particular Dream.

In the same way, at 'Out of a fabulous story We fashion an empire's glory': the national airs are suggested not as being peculiarly fabulous stories (although under the present government 'Rule Britannia' has been made the most foolish of all national boasts),[98] *but as examples of the things that*

---

[97] At the end of the autograph score of the '*Enigma*' *Variations,* Elgar translated the quotation as 'I essay much, I hope little, I ask nothing'—see Robert Anderson and Jerrold Northrop Moore (eds), *The Music Makers, The Spirit of England, With Proud Thanksgiving,* Elgar Complete Edition, 10 (Sevenoaks: Novello, 1986), pp. vii, xi (f.n. 12). On Elgar's use of the quotation see Brian Trowell, 'Elgar's Use of Literature', in Raymond Monk (ed.), *Edward Elgar: Music and Literature* (Aldershot: Scolar Press, 1993), pp. 182–326, esp. p. 213.

[98] There are several possible reasons for Elgar's feeling that 'the country was going to the dogs' under Asquith's Liberal government: firstly, the industrial unrest (including the national coal strike), unprecedented in its threatening quality and violent actions, and for many, probably including Elgar, made all the more worrying because of the rise of the Labour Party; secondly, the social and economic reforms of David Lloyd George, provoking a stand-off

'music makers' have achieved. One more reference may be explained:

"But on one man's soul it hath broken
A light that doth not depart;
And his look, or a word he hath spoken,
Wrought flame in another man's heart."

Here I have quoted the Nimrod Variation as a tribute to the memory of my friend, A.J.Jaeger: by this I do not mean to convey that his was the only soul on which light had broken or that his was the only word, or look that wrought 'flame in another man's heart'; but I do convey that amongst all the inept writing and wrangling about music his voice was clear, ennobling, sober and sane and for his help and inspiration I make this acknowledgement.

Elgar listed his quotations, both the self and external, in the order in which they appear. The self-quotations are: the 'Enigma' theme from the *Variations*; the 'Judgement' motive from *The Dream of Gerontius*; a quotation from *Sea Pictures*; 'Nimrod' from the *Variations*; quotations from the finale of the Second Symphony, the first and second movements of the Violin Concerto, and *The Apostles*; the motto from the First Symphony; and 'Novissima hora est' from *Gerontius*. The

---

with the House of Lords, with the government threatening to create many new peers to get its legislation through; thirdly, the new government plans to grant independence (or at least devolution) to Ireland. We might also note the growing German threat, intensified by the Balkan crisis 1912–1913 (as mentioned in Chapter 2). I am grateful to Bernard Porter for helping with this historical context and list of suggestions (in an email communication, 27 August 2022).

external quotations comprise snatches from 'Rule, Britannia', and 'La Marseillaise'.

Table 1: 'Borrowed' Themes in The Music Makers

Figure	Stanza number and text extract	Quotation	Opus no. of work from which quotation taken
6	(Prelude)	'Enigma' theme from the *Variations*	Op. 36
10.3	1: We are the music makers,/And we are the dreamers of dreams…	'Judgement' motive from *The Dream of Gerontius*	Op. 38
11.1 11.3	Wandering by lone sea breakers, And sitting by desolate streams…	'Sea Slumber' song *from Sea Pictures* 'Enigma' theme	Op. 37 Op. 36

18	...2:...We fashion an empire's glory...	'Rule, Britannia' (18.4) + 'La Marseillaise' (19.1, 25.11)	
51	...5:...But on one man's soul it hath broken,/A light that doth not depart;	'Nimrod' from the *Variations*	Op. 36
53	And his look, or a word he hath spoken,/Wrought flame in another man's heart.	Second Symphony (finale)	Op. 63
75	...7:...Of the glorious futures we see...	'Enigma' theme	Op. 36
76.2 76.4 77.1	...a little apart from ye; In our dreaming and our singing...	Violin Concerto (1st movement), 'Enigma' theme, Violin Concerto (2nd movement) and a motive from *The Apostles* combined	Op. 61 Op. 36 Op. 49
79	...8:...infinite morning/Intrepid you hear us cry...	First Symphony (motto theme)	Op. 55

| 101 | And a singer who sings no more. | 'Novissima hora est', from *Gerontius* | Op. 38 |

With the benefit of hindsight, Elgar's decision to quote from pre-existing materials may appear to have been an obvious choice, by dint of both the imagery of the words and historical precedent. However, Elgar's employment is quite different from any of the historical examples and must be regarded as one of his most impressive inspirations.

The use of pre-existent material is at least as old as notated music. The earliest examples of polyphony make use of plainchant in the form of *cantus firmi*, and by the time of the Renaissance such treatment is highly elaborate, as in the Masses of Dufay, Ockeghem and Josquin, where we can find examples of both external material (especially plainchant) and self-borrowings (especially chanson melody).[99] It is a characteristic of such examples, however, that the borrowed material is hidden in the web of polyphony: its purpose is to provide a concealed foundation for the polyphony, whether the *cantus firmus* is restricted to one voice (normally the tenor) or 'migrates' between voices. Some examples of borrowed material which are meant to be heard and recognised were also known to Elgar, such as Mozart's quotation from *Le nozze di Figaro* in *Don Giovanni* (one of

---

[99] Elgar acquired a knowledge of the Renaissance contrapuntal composers as a youth, through his copy of Friedrich Rochlitz's *Sammlung vorzüglicher Gesangstücke* (Mainz: B. Schotts Söhne, 1838); see Jerrold Northrop Moore, *Edward Elgar: A Creative Life* (Oxford University Press, 1987), p. 70.

the favourite examples of the earliest newspaper reviews of *The Music Makers*).[100] Examples which were probably not known to Elgar, but are much closer to his creation, are the first four symphonies (1888–1900) of Mahler which contain quotations from his songs, especially the collection *Des Knaben Wunderhorn*.[101] The most relevant example, and undoubtedly the prime motivation for Elgar's procedure, was Richard Strauss's tone-poem *Ein Heldenleben* (1898), which Elgar heard on 6 December 1902 at the Queen's Hall in a performance—the first one in England—conducted by the composer.

Even the above-named example of Strauss does not account for the inventiveness of Elgar, for in the Strauss, which is purely orchestral, the self-quotations are confined to a single section—'Des Helden Friedenswerke' ('The Hero's

---

[100] Mozart also quoted, in the same scene in *Don Giovanni*, from Martin y Soler's *Una cosa rara* and Giuseppi Sarti's *Fra i due litiganti il terzo gode.*

[101] Whilst there is no evidence that Elgar knew any music by Mahler, the latter came into direct contact with Elgar's music whilst on his second visit to New York as conductor of the New York Philharmonic Orchestra, when he conducted performances of the '*Enigma*' *Variations* (on 29 November and 2 December 1910) and four songs from *Sea Pictures* (on 14 and 17 February 1911). See the series of articles by Alexander Odefey: 'Edward Elgar and Gustav Mahler: The possibility of an encounter (part one)', *The Elgar Society Journal*, 20/1 (2017); 'Edward Elgar and Gustav Mahler: "who is virtually unknown in England" (part two)', *The Elgar Society Journal*, 20/2 (2017), pp. 17–37; 'Edward Elgar and Gustav Mahler: "the only man living who could do it" (part three),' *The Elgar Society Journal*, 20/3 (2017), pp. 25–50.

Works of Peace') —whereas Elgar's quotations are suggested by the words and are woven throughout the composition. In short, there is no shortage of historical precedent for the incorporation of borrowed material, but it is difficult to think of an example which goes anywhere near matching Elgar's procedure.

We will begin by tracing the use of the 'Enigma' theme.

The first quotation occurs approximately half way through the orchestral prelude (at figure 6), by which time the tonality has moved from the key of the Ode as a whole, F minor, into a passage of restless modulations, the first climax, and a gradual move to G minor, the key of the op. 36 *Variations*. As soft strings, woodwind and harp hover on an undulating semiquaver figure, violas, cellos, cor anglais and clarinets give the first rendition of the 'Enigma' theme, for a full twelve bars. For those listening sympathetically for the first time, the effect can perhaps be described as ethereal, a quality made more intense by the very unexpectedness of the occurrence. Repeated hearings hardly lessen the intensity. The theme is heard in triple time, as opposed to the quadruple time of the original, and the rhythms are varied somewhat accordingly, but the basic harmonic progressions are the same; in short, if we think back to the op. 36 *Variations*, this quotation continues the process of variation across both genre and time. A further, on this occasion brief, reference to the theme is heard five bars later, and then an even briefer reference (from figure 8.4).

The next reference occurs after the first choral entry, at the words, 'desolate streams'—now in the quadruple time of the original and very close rhythmically—and then again, just before the conclusion of stanza 1 (in F minor).

The 'Enigma' theme is next heard in stanza 7 (from figure 75), after a climactic passage and at the words 'Of the glorious futures we see', now in E flat minor. The woodwind render the theme in compound duple time, against one of the two contrapuntal themes which had formed the basis of the opening of stanza 7 (which was itself a reprise from stanza 3). After the choir sing poignantly (at figure 76) 'in our dreaming [minor mode] and our singing' [major mode] to the rhythm of the 'Enigma' theme, and with an enchanting 'A little apart from ye', we hear a final reference to the theme, along with quotations from the first and second movements of the Violin Concerto and *The Apostles* (from where Elgar provides a decorated version of the melody at the words 'There shall ye see him', from Part VI, perhaps hinting that truth and meaning are as likely to be found in 'dreaming' and 'singing' as in waking and speaking). In this passage between figure 75 and 77.5, we have the epitome of a dreamlike quality which Elgar has created for this work: fleeting images disappearing beyond our grasp.

In short, all the quotations of the 'Enigma' theme can be considered both in terms of their expressive significance as described by Elgar ('the loneliness of the artist') and as retrospective references to the op. 36 theme: how it can be further varied whilst retaining its recognisable character.

We will now look at the two quotations from *The Dream of Gerontius*, op. 38. The first comes at the conclusion of the second line of choral text, 'And we are the dreamers of dreams'. Coinciding with the word 'dreams' the strings and harp play a two-bar version of the very opening motive (labelled by Jaeger as the 'Judgement motive' of

Gerontius[102]) and here used with symbolic reference to the idea of dreams (but not with 'judgement' at this point).[103] In op. 38, the theme is at first presented as four bars of unaccompanied melody (played by violas, clarinets and bassoons), and then the opening two bars are harmonised with a first inversion chord, a German sixth and a dominant seventh in second inversion. In op. 69, the texture and sonority are different again yet retaining the characteristic German sixth.

The second quotation from op. 38 occurs at figure 101, in the last two bars of the soloist's part and the words 'in spite of a dreamer who slumbers, And a singer who sings no more' (beginning with F-sharp minor harmony, forming an

---

[102] See A.J. Jaeger, *Analytical and Descriptive Notes to* The Dream of Gerontius (London: Novello, 1900).

[103] The significance of dreams in Elgar's music can be observed not only in *The Dream of Gerontius* and *The Music Makers* but also in the lovely orchestral *Dream Children*, op. 43 (1902). Above the music of this last named piece, Elgar wrote a passage from Charles Lamb's essay from which Elgar's title is taken: 'And while I stood gazing, both the children gradually grew fainter to my view, receding, and still receding till nothing at last but two mournful features were seen in the uttermost distance, which, without speech, strangely impressed upon me the effects of speech: "We are not of Alice, nor of thee, nor are we children at all…We are nothing; less than nothing, and dreams. *We are only what might have been*"'; quoted in Moore, *Edward Elgar: A Creative Life*, p. 363. This idea of images appearing and then disappearing beyond grasp is apposite when considering the use of Elgar's quotations in *The Music Makers*. Elgar returned to the theme of dreams for the dream sequence in *Falstaff* (1913).

interrupted cadence from the previous chord). The source for this quotation is Gerontius's desperately moving 'Novissima hora est' (meaning 'My end is near', beginning with C-sharp minor harmony, forming an interrupted cadence from the previous chord) from Part I (from figure 66), and the symbolism for *The Music Makers* is this time both precise and relevant. The string sonority and effective chromatic harmony (reminiscent of so much of *Parsifal*) is retained (with the Elgarian octave doubling in the inner parts). As the soloist's words 'a singer who sings no more' are repeated and as she fades away, so is the quotation heard a final time (this time beginning in B minor).

The one and only quotation from *Sea Pictures* (from the song 'Sea Slumber') occurs mainly in the strings (with woodwind support), in conjunction with the words 'Wand'ring by lone sea-breakers, And sitting by desolate streams' (from figure 11); although this is only a brief reference to op. 37, the effective, evocative and felicitous qualities can hardly be overstated.

We now turn to the most extensive self-quotation in the entire work: the 'Nimrod' melody from the ninth variation of op. 36, Elgar's most passionate tribute to his late friend, adviser, and advocate. The words at which the quotation appears (from figure 51) could hardly be more apposite: 'But on one man's soul it hath broken, a light that doth not depart'. In both op. 36 and op. 69 the Nimrod sections form the main expressive climax of each work—in op. 36 the variation begins roughly two thirds of the way in and in op. 69 the equivalent passage begins roughly half way in. In other words, just as the *Variations* owe their popularity as much to the 'Nimrod' variation as to any other part, so the Nimrod section and what immediately follows can probably claim pre-eminence as the most absorbing, deeply moving passage in the entire *Music Makers*.

In *The Music Makers* the orchestral music at the 'Nimrod' section is at first almost identical with the equivalent point in the *Variations*, one obvious difference being the countermelody provided by the vocal soloist, which follows the broad contours of the melody but with its own rhythmic life and melodic shape, and with a *fermata* in the second bar, on the word 'man's'. This vocal line also exploits with great subtlety several opportunities for word painting, especially at 'it hath broken' (insertion of a rest), and 'A light' (sustained melodic climax).

The tempo and quality of this passage changed during the thirteen years which separated composition of the *Variations* and *The Music Makers*. In the autograph score of 1899, the 'Nimrod' Variation is headed 'Moderato' (crotchet = 66), but in 1903, having reconsidered the matter, Elgar asked Jaeger to change the marking in the printed full score (first published by Novello in 1899) to *Adagio* and a metronome mark of crotchet = 52.[104] By the time of *The Music Makers,* the tempo indication has slowed down even further to crotchet = *circa* 46, and the passage is marked *solenne*. As pointed out by Julian Rushton, Elgar is reinterpreting his own music to lend

---

[104] Letter written from Malvern on 17 September 1903; Percy M. Young (ed.) *Letters to Nimrod: Edward Elgar to August Jaeger 1897–1908* (London: Dobson, 1965), pp. 211–212. See also Robert Anderson, Jerrold Northrop Moore (eds), *Elgar Complete Edition: Op. 36 Variations on an Original Theme for Orchestra* (London and Sevenoaks: Novello, 1986), pp. x, xi and xviii.

a more elegiac quality in tribute to his departed friend.[105] Then comes the main, obvious departure from the original Nimrod passage: in op. 36 the music continued in E flat, but in op. 69 there occurs a modulation to A flat, by turns moving and transformative. Coinciding with this modulation the choir enters (at figure 52) with a rich variation on the theme, providing a choral counterpoint to the equally rich orchestral texture. As the music reaches 'man's heart', we have one of the most moving climaxes in the entire work, as soloist and choir overlap with their words, and at the *allargando* peroration we are transported (at figure 53.1) imperceptibly but magnificently to the finale of the Second Symphony: the great climactic point from figures 143.7 and 165 in the Symphony. In other words, the 'Nimrod' passage represents both a variation of a variation and one of Elgar's greatest inspirations.

This juxtaposition of 'Nimrod' and the Second Symphony quotations is an extraordinary stroke. Not only does the Second Symphony theme have a motivic, unifying resemblance with the second *ritornello*,[106] in its melodic descents of diminished and perfect fifths, but it also expresses another moving tribute, this time to the memory of King

---

[105] Julian Rushton, *Elgar*: '*Enigma' Variations* (Cambridge University Press, 1999), p. 46. As further pointed out by Prof. Rushton (in the same place), Elgar continued with this slower tempo for 'Nimrod' in his 1926 recording of the *Variations*. See also Jerrold Northrop Moore, *Elgar on Record: The Composer and the Gramophone* (Oxford University Press, 1974), p. 60.

[106] Elgar's use of what I term *ritornelli* is described in the passage headed *Ritornelli* below.

Edward VII,[107] as we remember Elgar's dedication as it appears in the first edition of the full score of the Second Symphony:

Dedicated to the memory of His late Majesty King Edward VII. This Symphony, designed early in 1910 to be a loyal tribute, bears its present dedication with the gracious approval of His Majesty, the King.[108]

There are two more self-quotations to consider. A quotation from the first movement of the Violin Concerto (from figure 17 of the Concerto) appears at the words 'A little apart from ye; in our dreaming, and our singing' (figure 76.2) and is combined with a tiny snatch (in woodwind) of the 'Enigma' theme. Was Elgar at this point symbolising romantic feelings for Alice Stuart Wortley (the Windflower), whose themes are abundant in the Concerto, who was destined to remain unattainable ('a little apart')? The answer appears to be a resounding affirmative, especially in view of his declaration in August that 'I think of you in the music',[109] and thus represents some of the clearest evidence of the depth of feelings for his muse. There is also a snatch, in the strings, from the second movement (from figure 55.3 of the Concerto) at figure 77.1 onwards, at the words 'In our dreaming, and our singing', soon to be combined with an elaborated version, in

---

[107] I am grateful to Natalie Marshall who offered this suggestion during a talk I gave to the North West branch of the Elgar Society on 28 May 2022.

[108] Robert Anderson, Jerrold Northrop Moore (eds), Symphony No. 2: Op. 63, Elgar Complete Edition, (Sevenoaks: Novello, 1984).

[109] Letter to Alice Stuart Wortley, quoted in Jerrold Northrop Moore, *The Windflower Letters* (Oxford University Press, 1989), p. 104.

flute and clarinet, of 'There [i.e. in your dreams] ye shall see him' from *The Apostles,* bringing stanza 6 to a conclusion.

The quotation from the first movement of the First Symphony occurs at the words 'And out of the infinite morning Intrepid you hear us cry' (figure 79), where the music builds up to the grandest expressive, dynamic marking in the entire work—*molto allargando* to *fff*—yet the textures are organised so that the choir is never overwhelmed by the orchestra and that consequently the words can be heard clearly.

Elgar acknowledged two external quotations: snatches of 'Rule, Britannia' and 'La Marseillaise'. He may have known of Beethoven's incorporation of the first of these patriotic songs in *Wellingtons Sieg* ('Battle Symphony'), op. 91, and Tchaikovsky's incorporation of the second in the '1812 Overture', op. 49, and Schumann's in *Faschingsschwank aus Wien*, op. 26; he may also have noticed Sullivan's employment of national airs in some of the Savoy operas. Though Elgar's use is equally redolent of the Beethoven and Tchaikovsky examples, is it possible that the source of the *irony* was Sullivan?[110] In *The Music Makers* the quotations

---

[110] On the relationship between Elgar and Sullivan, see Meinhard Saremba, '"…Unconnected with the schools"—Edward Elgar and Arthur Sullivan', *The Elgar Society Journal*, 17/4 (2012), pp. 4–23. Elgar's penchant for the Savoy operas is evidenced by his attendance at *The Yeoman of the Guard* on 7 May 1889, *The Sorcerer* and *Trial by Jury* on 18 October 1898, and *Iolanthe* on 22 February 1902, as well as his enthusiasm for leading the band in an 1891 performance of *The Pirates of Penzance* at Settle; sources: Martin Bird (ed.), *Edward Elgar: Collected Correspondence* (Elgar Works), V/1 (2013), *Provincial Musician: Diaries 1857–1896,* p.

coincide with the words from stanza 2, 'We fashion an Empire's Glory' (from figure 17.8). Regarding the opening of the British song ('When Britain first at...') it is perhaps significant that Elgar breaks off the quotation before 'Heaven's Command', in view of his disgust at Asquith's Liberal government, and that the melody appears (satirically, ironically?) rhythmically distorted, in cor anglais, horns and violas, before the French national anthem snippet appears, in trumpets (at 19.1), as the chorus climaxes at the words 'We fashion an empire's glory', played by trumpets—and so considerably easier to hear than the 'Rule, Britannia' snippet.

In summary, Elgar's manner of incorporating quotations, especially self-borrowings, is both masterly and highly original. In some cases, the self-quotations can be thought of as variations of pre-existent material, or, in the case of the 'Nimrod' passage, a variation of a variation.

Ritornelli

The orchestral prelude contains two main themes (Ex. 1a, 1b). The first, for strings, woodwind, brass and timpani—very loud and marked *espressivo appassionato*, and in the home

---

29, V/2 (2015), *Road to Recognition*: *Diaries 1897–1901*, p. 129, V/3 (2016), *The Path to Knighthood*: *Diaries 1902–1904*, pp. 17–18; Moore, *Edward Elgar: Letters of a Lifetime* (Oxford University Press, 1990), p. 37. Although we do not know if Elgar ever attended a performance of *Utopia Limited*, which contains the most numerous satirical references to 'Rule, Britannia' of all the Savoy operas, he could have looked at the vocal score published by Chappell and Co. in 1893 (as pointed out by Meinhard Saremba in an email, 1 September 2022).

key of F minor—is restless and searching, qualities emphasised by the chromatic accompaniment: the kind of chromaticism found in many passages of Wagner's *Parsifal* (with which Elgar was familiar, having studied it carefully prior to witnessing performances in Bayreuth on 28 July and 1 August 1892). From the evidence of sketches probably from 1912,[111] Elgar tried out the theme both with and without the introductory sustained unison F, low in pitch, similar in manner to the unison openings of the First Symphony, *The Apostles* and *The Kingdom*. In *The Music Makers,* the device is accompanied by a big crescendo and sense of drama before the first theme unfolds, rather like the opening of *The Apostles*. This has the effect of a dramatic opening, and also facilitates good ensemble, which would have been more difficult with an anacrusis opening. The second theme (at figure 2) begins in F minor but continues in the relative major, in lower strings accompanied by woodwind and harp; marked at the outset *pianissimo dolce*, this theme, in contrast to the opening one, is soft and pleading in quality but builds up to an impressive 'climax' in its ninth bar.[112]

Both themes recur throughout the Ode, often in different keys, and play a crucial role, not only expressively but structurally in highlighting major divisions in the music. In these senses, they are not entirely remote from the device of *ritornelli* as found in arias and concertos of the Baroque and

---

[111] British Library, Add MS 47908, and MS Mus. 1843/1/6; this second sketch is headed 'The Complete Understanding' and was sent to Alice Stuart Wortley on 15 May 1912.

[112] Elgar labelled this bar 'climax' in the sketch sent to Alice Stuart Wortley on 15 May 1912, MS Mus. 1843/1/6.

Classical eras (with examples by Vivaldi, Bach, Handel, Haydn, Mozart, Beethoven and countless other composers) — and so, we will label them Ritornello A and Ritornello B. The table below shows the occurrences of these *ritornelli.*

Table 2: Appearances of the Ritornelli

Fig.	Description	Comments	Key
	Ritornello A	Begins after pedal note F	f
2	Ritornello B		f/A flat
14.4	Ritornello A	Appears at the end of stanza 1, followed by an agitated passage leading into stanza 2	f
36.2	Ritornello A	Appears at the end of stanza 2	b flat-f
38	Ritornello B	Leads into stanza 3, and continues as voices pick out the main contours of the melody	f/A flat
50	Ritornello B	First in orchestra and then in voice with orchestra, leading to the 'Nimrod' section at fig. 51	f/A flat Modulating

67.7	Ritornello A	Appearing at the end of stanza 6	f (over dom. pedal)
82	Ritornello A	Leading to the last two lines of stanza 8	c
88	Ritornello B	Orchestra and soloist	b flat/D flat—A flat
93	Ritornello B	Appears with the chorus and then the soloist	a/C Modulating and again reaching A flat
99	Ritornello B	Appears as a fragment with the soloist	b flat
101.3	Ritornello A	Appearing with chorus and the *Gerontius* 'Novissima' (f sharp and b) and ending with single note E, before final choral utterance	b-e

Refrains

Another recurring element is the refrain which sets the opening two lines: 'We are the music makers, And we are the dreamers of dreams' (Ex. 2a). This was entirely Elgar's idea, O'Shaughnessy's poem having no such recurrences, and gives to the setting another layer of unity and expressiveness. The first, second and final statements of the Refrain are soft and centre on F minor, providing an ethereal quality tinged with sadness. In contrast, the central statements (at figures 60 and 64.7) are climactic and thrilling. The longest passage without the Refrain is between the penultimate and final statements, and the effect here will be considered further in the discussion of tonality.

Table 3: Refrains

Figure	Refrain	Comment	Key
10	'We are the music makers,/And we are the dreamers of dreams'	Chorus, first entry	f
37.1	'(We are the music makers, And we are the dreamers of dreams)'	Appears at the end of stanza 4, against Ritornello A	b flat/f over dom. pedal
60	'(We are the music makers, And we are the dreamers of dreams)'	Appears at the end of stanza 6, at the end of a massive climax, and followed by another setting of stanza 6	b flat
64.7	'(We are the movers and shakers Of the world forever, it seems)'	A partial transposition of the previous Refrain, followed by more of stanza 6	c
103	'We are the music makers/And we are the dreamers of dreams'	Final statement of the Refrain	f

Leitmotiven?

For some listeners at early performances of *The Music Makers*, the themes, especially the 'borrowed' ones, would have been suggestive of *Leitmotiven*, meaning 'leading motives.'[113] As is well known, these are especially associated with the operas of Wagner, such as *Der Ring des Nibelungen, Tristan und Isolde* and *Parsifal,* in which recurring themes, harmonies, or rhythms are connected with characters, emotions, situations or ideas. Jaeger undoubtedly encouraged such associations in Elgar's choral music through his analytical essays, in which he identified a large number of leading motives for each of *The Dream of Gerontius, The Apostles* and *The Kingdom* oratorios.[114] Both Charles Maclean, writing in December 1912,[115] and the unnamed reviewer in *The Musical Times* (1 November 1912) appeared to take for granted that the 'borrowed' themes in *The Music Makers* qualified as *Leitmotiven*:

---

[113] A recent thorough treatment of the subject is Florian Csizmadia, *Leitmotivik und verwandte Techniken in den Chorwerken von Edward Elgar: Analysen und Kontexte* (Berlin: Verlag Dr Köster, 2017).

[114] Jaeger, *Analytical Notes to* The Dream of Gerontius, The Apostles, *and* The Kingdom (London: Novello, 1900, 1903, 1906).

[115] Charles Maclean, Review of *The Music Makers* in the *Zeitschrift der internationalen Musikgesellschaft*, December 1912; an extensive quotation is given in Chapter 2.

...the leitmotives are so ingeniously and naturally dovetailed onto their environment as never to obtrude, and they always seem to fit the situation to a nicety.[116]

Ernest Newman used the term, but only once, in his analytical essay, when he describes the whole-tone scale—heard at the lines 'Can trample a kingdom down' (figure 25), 'And o'erthrew them' (figure 30.7) and 'That ye of the past must die' (figure 83.1)—as 'a sort of leitmotif of morality'.

On the other hand, none of the early newspaper critics made explicit use of the term and nor did Elgar (whose enthusiasm for labelling motives fell well short of Jaeger's, despite Elgar's knowledge of the *Ring, Tristan* and *Parsifal*). Nevertheless, the 'borrowed' themes inevitably carry *Leitmotiv* suggestions, if only retrospectively: the Enigma theme represents, in Elgar's own words, 'the loneliness of the Artist'; the 'Novissima hora est' quotation (from *Gerontius*) had already been labelled by Jaeger as 'Judgement' (although that particular association would not be appropriate at this point); and the quotations from *Sea Pictures*, and the Second and First Symphonies may suggest *Leitmotiven* such as 'the sea', 'passion', 'courage', all of which are relevant to the words at those points. The two *ritornelli* may also be suggestive: Elgar himself described the second one in a sketch (but without using the word *Leitmotiv*) as 'with perfect joy'

---

[116] 'The Birmingham Music Festival', in *The Musical Times*, 53, no. 837 (1 November 1912), p. 724; a more extensive extract is quoted in chapter 2.

(although whether this is a *Leitmotive*-type indication, or a conceptual performance direction is not clear).[117]

In short, whilst there is some evidence of *Leitmotiv* connection around the time of first performance, today's interpreters and listeners are likely to be divided between those who find such labels helpful, and those who find that the reflective, rather than narrative, nature of the Ode militates against the very concept.

Symphonic Elements

It is clear from the title page of the autograph vocal score that Elgar considered various descriptions for the work, including 'Symphony for Chorus and Orchestra', before settling on the final title of *The Music Makers*.[118] We recall from Chapter 1 that Elgar had made reference to similar terminology in connection with *The Black Knight* (1893), which he described in a letter to Jaeger (1898) as 'a sort of symphony', and in the preface to the reissued vocal score

---

[117] London, British Library, MS. Mus. 1843/1/6, dated 15 May 1912, and sent to Alice Stuart Wortley.

[118] London, British Library, Add. MS. 58036. As described in Chapter 1, the front cover (written by Elgar in black ink) reads:
To my friend/Nicholas Kilburn/Doctor of Music [crossed out]/The Music Makers/Ode [added later]/by Arthur O'Shaughnessy/Set to music/for Chorus [deleted] Contralto Solo Chorus [added above and positioned with a caret] and/orchestra/by/Edward Elgar/Op. 69/[The following crossed out] Symphony/for solo, chorus and orchestra/The Music Makers/An Ode/by/Elgar.

(1898) as 'symphonic in design'.[119] Suggestions were made by Percy Young for analysing the work in terms of a possible symphonic construction,[120] with the opening up to figure 49 representing the equivalent of a symphonic first movement, the section beginning with the solo vocal entry (marked *Lento*) representing a second (slow?) movement, the passage from figure 55 a lively third movement (*scherzo*?), and from figure 78 (the return of F minor and a varied Refrain) a finale. For some listeners, such analytical divisions may be helpful, but there are too many contradictions of tempi and thematic recall for such neat divisions to be entirely convincing—no doubt as Elgar came to appreciate when settling on his final title of *The Music Makers*. Moreover, as will be discussed later, the tonal scheme of the whole is rather different from what one might expect in a symphonic work. On the other hand, there are clearly symphonic elements in this choral

---

[119] Julian Rushton, '*The Black Knight*: Elgar's first Symphony?', *The Elgar Society Journal*, 22/5 (2021), pp. 1–13.

[120] Percy M. Young, *Elgar O.M.: A Study of a Musician*, 2nd edition (London and New York: White Lion Publishers, 1973), p. 305. Young's views about a possible symphonic structure are further discussed and elaborated by Aiden J. Thomson, 'Unmaking *The Music Makers*', in *Elgar Studies*, ed. J.P.E. Harper-Scott and Julian Rushton (Cambridge University Press, 2007), pp. 99–134; Thomson proceeds to offer an alternative model—see pp. 108 ff. Yet another model is proposed by Florian Csizmadia, with a division of the work into Introduction, Part 1, Transition, Parts 2 and 3, Transition and beginning of Reprise, Part 4, Part 5 (Finale), and Epilogue, but this division raises as many difficulties as Young's but in different ways—see *Leitmotivik und verwandte Techniken in den Chorwerken von Edward Elgar*, p. 481.

work—just as there are in the masses of Haydn, Mozart or Beethoven, the motets and masses of Bruckner, or countless other examples, including *The Dream of Gerontius, The Apostles* and *The Kingdom*. These symphonic elements include thematic and tonal contrasts, changes of tempi, development, and return, of thematic material, a full range of expressive devices, vivid and brilliant orchestration, incorporation of solo and choral voices with the orchestral texture, and a sense of the grandiose in many passages, contrasting with the most intimate expression.

Vocal Parts and Word Setting

One advantage of the relative brevity of the text—consisting of 9 stanzas of 8 lines each—and its reflective rather than narrative quality is that Elgar was able to dwell on passages, repeat them, intertwine them with orchestral textures, treat the solo part as melody with accompaniment or as counterpoint to orchestral or choral textures. These features stand somewhat in contrast to the much larger-scale *Scenes from the Saga of King Olaf* (1896) or *Caractacus* (1898), where the lengthy, narrative text offers less opportunity for extensive repetition because of the need to 'make progress' with the words, especially in the case of *King Olaf*.[121] The situation is different again for the three big oratorios—*The Dream of Gerontius*, *The Apostles* and *The Kingdom*—whose scale is also vast compared with *The Music Makers*.

---

[121] The main exception is the exquisite setting of the words 'As torrents in summer', in *King Olaf*, where time seems to stand still, and which remains by far the best (and for many listeners only) known passage in the entire work.

The first choral entry is one of Elgar's greatest masterstrokes. After the very substantial orchestral prelude with its wide range of expression, thematic contrast, and self-quotation, the music dies away leaving only harp and violins on two notes: tonic and third of F minor. After a silence, the choir enter serenely, virtually unaccompanied, and, as it were, introduce themselves: 'We are the music makers, And we are the dreamers of dreams' (Exs 2a, 2b). In terms of dramatic timing, expression and effect, it is difficult to think of a more striking example of scene setting in the whole of Elgar's oeuvre.

The choral writing is challenging,[122] but in a stimulating rather than discouraging way with all parts equal, employing a wide tessitura and varied functions and styles. Elgar's employment of the choir—sometimes *a cappella*, sometimes accompanied, at other times in antiphony with the orchestra, accompanying the orchestra or being accompanied by it—is evidence of a master at work. A few more examples must suffice.

At figure 27, as the harmony sinks by semitone, in two-bar units—C natural—B natural—B flat—A natural—at the words 'We, in the ages lying In the buried past of the earth', the choir are in unison whilst the instruments play in contrary motion, and then, at the words 'Built Nineveh with our

---

[122] An unidentified newspaper review following the Brighton Festival performance on 13 November 1912 perhaps encapsulates the level of difficulty: 'The technique of the choir was severely strained, but never to breaking point...Much of the music is very difficult, especially some of the entries, but on the whole careful training and familiarity with the music...won the day.'

sighing', their unison singing continues, strikingly, in the Dorian mode, bringing an antique flavour to the whole, which is highly appropriate for the biblical reference.

There are further references to an antique style—for example at figure 32, at the words 'To the old of the new world's worth; For each age is a dream that is dying', where the chorus breaks climactically into a passage of double counterpoint—that is, with two subjects treated contrapuntally; on the evidence of a sketchbook, this passage may have been at first intended for *The Dream of Gerontius*.[123] The contrapuntal passage reappears from figure 71, now to the words 'With our dreaming and singing, Ceaseless and sorrowless we' and softer and a little slower, but building up climactically. This repetition, along with the two *ritornelli* and the frequent references to the 'Enigma' theme, further strengthen the sense of unity in the work as a whole.

The solo contralto is not heard until about half way through the work (Ex. 4a). The effect may be likened to a delayed entry in a Shakespeare play or Mozart opera (such as that of the Countess in *Le nozze di Figaro*, who does not appear until the beginning of Act 2): the effect in those examples and here is all the more striking for the delay. Moreover, just as Elgar had set the scene so effectively for the initial entry of the chorus (as described above) so he sets the scene for the initial entry of his soloist. From figures 46 to 49, we have one of the most stable and harmonically bright passages in the entire Ode: thirty-one bars centred on G major, anchored with a pedal-note G, as orchestra and chorus wind

---

[123] London, British Library, Add. MS. 47902, p. 9 (215).

down, eventually leaving only divided violas and harp with a G major triad, which switches at the last moment to a G minor triad (by dint of a single change of note in upper violas). Magnificently, the scene is now set.

Elgar's choice of where to bring in his soloist was apposite, for at stanza 5, through stanza 6, the poetic voice changes from 'we' to 'they'—as in 'They had no vision amazing Of the goodly house they are raising'—and so the soloist acts as a narrator somewhat apart from the collective of music makers. Appropriately for this role as commentator, the style at this point (figure 49.1) is *quasi recitativo*, and Elgar soon brings in orchestral music heard earlier (at figure 27), as the tonality changes expressively from G minor to E flat for the extended 'Nimrod' section (Ex. 4b).

Here, in probably the most moving passage, the soloist outlines, or even 'caresses', the main contours of the melody, mingling with the music makers, sometimes taking the lead, at other times doubling, reinforcing, or, at the point where reference is made to the Second Symphony (figure 53 onwards), providing a distinct melodic climax at possibly the expressive core of the entire work.

The agitated style of stanza 6 lends to the music a new dimension as soloist and chorus, punctuated energetically by the orchestra, drive the music to a massive climax, culminating in a Refrain for choir alone of 'We are the movers and shakers Of the world for ever, it seems.' (At this point, Elgar makes a virtue of necessity by concealing the poetically weak line-ending of 'it seems', with a strong overlap into the *Maestoso* section at figure 65.)

Notably at figure 65 Elgar treats the voices instrumentally in another climatic, contrapuntal passage, when the tenors, followed by sopranos, then basses and then altos leap up a minor seventh via an *appoggiatura* on the upper note, rather like a string *portamento*, giving to the voices a cutting edge which is nothing short of visceral; the device provides choral singers with an especially challenging yet satisfying moment.

The word setting for stanza 9 is much more flexible than it was earlier. Elgar sets stanzas 1–8 in the order in which O'Shaughnessy had left them, but in stanza 9 (from figure 85) the composer adopts a fluid manner so that we experience recalls from stanza 7 and 8 simultaneously with words from stanza 9.

Table 4: Text setting of stanza 9/7/8

Figure	Stanza number and text	Description
85	9: Great hail! We cry to the comers/From the dazzling unknown shore;/	Contralto solo. Ritornello B
88	Bring us hither your sun and your summers,/And renew our world as of yore;/	Contralto solo. Ritornello B
92	7: The glory about you clinging/Of the glorious futures you see,/Your souls with high music ringing:/	Contralto solo with chorus. Text from stanza 7 is interspersed with text from stanza 9 in a fluid manner.
92.19	7: O men! It must ever be/That we dwell in our dreaming and	Chorus with more text from stanza 7 interspersed with text

	singing,/A little apart from ye.	from stanza 9 in a fluid manner.
95	9: You shall teach us your song's new numbers,/And things that we dreamed not before:/	Soloist overlapping chorus in a flexible manner.
96.9 97.7	**8**: For we are afar with the dawning/ **9**: And renew our world as of yore/	Words from stanza 8 (in the chorus) sung simultaneously with words from stanza 9 (by the soloist)

This fluidity in the text setting has the effect of interrupting the original flow of O'Shaughnessy's text in order to recall ideas from earlier in his Ode—'The glory about you clinging, of the glorious futures you see, Your souls with high music singing' (soloist, from stanza 7) and 'Oh men! It must ever be That we dwell in our dreaming and singing, A little apart from ye' (chorus, from stanza 7)—followed climactically with the simultaneous rendition of 'For we are afar with the dawning' (chorus, from stanza 8), with 'And renew our world as of yore' (soloist, from stanza 9). At figure 98, the chorus continues with their text from stanza 8—'for we are afar with the dawning'—whilst the soloist picks up the words from stanza 9, 'You shall teach us', and joins the melody of the sopranos one bar late at a climactic point marked *poco allargando.* Throughout this extended passage the soloist stands apart, continuing the references to 'you', whilst the chorus continue as a collective, referring, as usual in this work, to 'we'. However, the soloist's joining in with the sopranos' melody, after a short delay, signals unity of thought from different perspectives.

I would like to offer one possible source for Elgar's idea of fluid text setting towards the end of the Ode, including simultaneous setting of different lines: the finale of Beethoven's Symphony no. 9. Towards the end of the Ninth, Beethoven's setting of Schiller's Ode *An die Freude* ('To Joy') becomes increasingly fluid and flexible in the selection and order of verses, a process which climaxes at the point (from bar 730 onwards) at which Beethoven combines lines from the first verse of Schiller's Ode ('Freude, schöner Götterfunken', etc. ('Joy, beautiful spark of the gods', etc.)) with lines from chorus 1 ('Seid umschlungen, Millionen!' ('Be embraced, you millions!')) in order to present simultaneously two related ideas.[124] In similar manner, Elgar's combing of earlier and later lines from O'Shaughnessy results in an accumulation of complexity and fluidity both poetically and musically leading to a sense of synthesis. Whether Elgar was aware of any such similarity of approach is unascertainable, but it is at least possible, even likely, that his vast experience may have resulted in such influence, whether consciously or subconsciously.[125]

---

[124] For a description of Beethoven's flexible arrangement of Schiller's text see David Young, *Beethoven Symphonies Revisited: Performance, Expression and Impact* (Brighton, Chicago, Toronto: Sussex Academic Press, 2021, 2022), pp. 208–217.

[125] Elgar had heard a performance of Beethoven's Ninth Symphony as recently as September 1911 at the Worcester Festival; see Moore, *Edward Elgar: A Creative Life,* p. 624.

At the start of stanza 9 (figure 85), after two and a half bars of agitated orchestral sounds, especially in the strings, the soloist returns with the words 'Great hail! we cry to the comers From the dazzling unknown shore'.[126] Using at this point the *appoggiatura/portamento* device used by the chorus earlier (from figure 65), she soon reaches her vocal climax with a top G, against which Elgar provides, in small notes, a lower alternative which no singer worth her salt would consider using as the effect is so much weaker.

Figure 85.2 onwards represents the longest section for soloist without chorus. After her climactic passage, she joins the strings in an extended passage based on Ritornello B (from figure 88), at first following the broad contours of the melody and then providing a countermelody at 'You shall teach us your song's new numbers.' The tension mounts at figure 92, over a pedal G (as dominant of C major), and cries out for relief at the words, repeated from stanza 7, 'The glory about you clinging Of the glorious futures you see', leading to the *allargando* climax at 'Your souls with high music ringing' in C major (again from stanza 7), with the soloist highlighting the third of the chord. Here, Elgar alters the grammar of O'Shaughnessy's Ode from the first-person plural (heard earlier at figure 70.5 onwards) to the second-person plural, probably in order to retain his demarcation between the collective of music makers, who refer to themselves as 'we', and the commentator (the soloist), who refers to them as 'you' or 'ye', a subtlety which can easily be overlooked, but which

---

[126] Elgar's early thought, on the evidence of a sketch, was to have a bar of orchestral unison crescendo before the agitated figuration at figure 85: London, British Library, Add. MS. 63159, f. 5A9.

deserves to be celebrated for the imaginative stroke which it is.

At this point (one bar before figure 93) the chorus enters at the final note of the solo passage, singing words from stanza 8 in chords with the fundamental melodic notes of Ritornello B and its harmonies—i.e. the first note of each bar—to the words: 'O men! It must ever be That we dwell, in our dreaming and singing, A little apart from ye', a deceptively simple passage, overwhelming in its effect. At 95, the soloist re-enters with a repeat of 'You shall teach us' (from stanza 9).

In short, the increased flexibility of word setting in stanza 9 not only results in an accumulation of complexity, as different but related thoughts are expressed simultaneously, but also expands the scale of this section and delays the entry of the final two lines of the Ode—'Yea in spite of a dreamer who slumbers, And a singer who sings no more.' This expanding of the length of the work as a whole into a forty-minute total, as opposed to what would have been around thirty-five minutes had the word recalls and combinations not been there, can only have been advantageous in meeting the expectations of a commission for a major festival.[127] In other words, as so often happens in the creative fields, artistic and pragmatic considerations coalesce in perfect harmony.

Orchestral Writing

Elgar scores his Ode for a large orchestra: piccolo, 2 flutes, 2 oboes, cor anglais, 2 clarinets in B flat, bass clarinet in B flat, 2 bassoons, contra bassoon, 4 horns in F, 3 trumpets

---

[127] I am grateful to Julian Rushton for this observation (in an email communication, 18 November 2022).

in B flat, 3 trombones, tuba, 3 kettle drums tuned F, C, E flat, percussion (cymbals, bass drum, triangle, side drum, the same combination he had used in the *'Enigma' Variations*), 2 harps, organ, and strings (2 violins, violas, cellos and double basses). Elgar's use of percussion here is perhaps reminiscent of the military associations of such instruments in a large number of Classical works, including Haydn's 'Military' Symphony and Beethoven's Ninth Symphony, although the percussion are used more discreetly in the Elgar.

Anyone familiar with Elgar's large-scale works up to this point—especially the *'Enigma' Variations*, oratorios, symphonies and Violin Concerto—would not be surprised to discover the masterly way in which he uses the orchestra, in this case to reflect the words, sometimes in ways which enhance O'Shaughnessy's conceits but at other times which appear to suggest different shades of meaning, as will be demonstrated in the following selected examples and later in the full analysis.

The work begins with some of the lower wind, kettle drum and strings on unison F with a crescendo leading to the opening impassioned statement of Ritornello A for full orchestra (except percussion, harp and organ), providing a full-blooded announcement of the highly emotional character of the work. With the entry of Ritornello B, the theme is given to violas and cellos in unison, in a manner familiar from Beethoven—as in the slow movement of the Fifth Symphony. The harp accompaniment though is a distinctly Elgarian touch, calling to mind exquisite passages from his First Symphony. The way in which the passage builds up to an impassioned climax aided by the accumulation of instruments is evidence of a master at work. As the scene is set for the entry of the chorus, the orchestration is reduced to nothing more than violins and harp, the long silence exquisitely producing an ethereal, unforgettable moment.

Virtually 'a cappella', the first choral entry is followed by the first 'Gerontius' quotation delicately scored for strings, harps, kettle drum and horns, and soon after the harps word-paint the 'desolate streams' with shimmering *glissandi.* At the end of the massive build-up to the words 'shakers of the world' loud triplets in the brass shake at least the concert hall.

The way in which the two externally-borrowed themes 'Rule, Britannia' and 'La Marseillaise' are concealed in the middle of the texture at the words 'We fashion an empire's glory'—the first quotation in cor anglais, horns and strings, the second on one trumpet—raises the question of how clearly Elgar wanted the themes to be heard, for even the 'Marseillaise' quotation could easily be missed, and the 'Rule, Britannia' would hardly be noticed at all, were it not for Elgar's pointing it out in his Note (as described earlier in this chapter). Another brief reference to 'Marseillaise', occurring between figures 25.11 and 26, should be pointed out as it would probably otherwise escape notice, despite being sung and with the rhythm reinforced by trombones and side drum. This is the most militaristic image of all, the words being 'And three with a new song's measure Can trample a kingdom down', where the message is drummed home literally by kettle drum and percussion (with a rhythmic figure which is virtually identical to the one which opens *Caractacus* (as mentioned in Chapter 1)). Another quasi-imperialistic message is sounded—but more subtly, with a sinister edge, as if from a distance—that the 'multitudes are enlisted In the faith that their fathers resisted' (from figure 56).

The organ is used sparingly, sometimes to reinforce climaxes, at other times to support delicate passages, such as providing an 8-foot sonority when double basses and contra bassoon are absent, or in a different function, as at figures 32 and 71, where the instrument has all the contrapuntal lines and acts as additional support for the voices. The organ, however, is never a lone voice or accompaniment and performances can take place without it, though its presence undoubtedly adds an additional, subtle layer.

From the many examples of delicate string scoring, we may cite the filigree passage from figure 42, at the words 'of our dreaming Unearthly impossible seeming', which is so suited to solo violin that one wonders why Elgar did not score it that way, right up to figure 43.4. When the strings alone play the 'Nimrod' theme at figure 51, the full, rich sonority (as mentioned earlier) is virtually identical with that part of the work from which it was extracted, at least for the first six bars, but with the double basses playing a reduced role, reserving full support for the choral entry at figure 52.

At other times, woodwind solos appear as if from nowhere to produce the most delicate sensations, as in the tiny clarinet solo at figure 39.4.

One of the most extraordinary examples of Elgar's skill as an orchestrator not only provides a thrilling climax but makes a virtue of a weak line ending in O'Shaughnessy's poetry. This (at figure 65) has already been commented on, but the orchestration demands more detailed attention. '…Of the world for ever, it seems': 'it seems' is taken over the bar line and set to a huge *tutti* with each of the woodwind and brass sections, harps and organ harmonically complete, the strings driving the music forwards, and the choral voices overlapping with the phrase-end in a new line of text: 'The multitudes are bringing to pass the dream'. Here, effective word setting, melody, harmony, rhythm, and orchestration interact at the highest artistic level.

Perhaps the most resourceful passage of instrumentation in the entire work occurs at figure 82 onwards, notably the sensational semiquavers in trombones and lower woodwind and lower strings, with the rest of the woodwind and strings soon joining in, as the dramatic warning is given ('That ye of the past must die'). At other times we notice trumpets emerging at the top of a texture, or delicately supporting a vocal line.

Further examples of Elgar's brilliant orchestration will be given as the analyses progress, but for the time being it is worth noting that Elgar follows the principles of the great symphonic composers of the nineteenth century, especially Schumann, Brahms and Dvorak, in ensuring a firm harmonic foundation for his orchestral sonorities, so that in the *tutti* sections each of the main groups—woodwind, brass and kettle drums, strings—is harmonically complete and self-contained. From many possible examples, we may cite the climactic passage at figure 46, with its choirs of woodwind, brass and kettle drum, strings, organ, and voices. However varied, subtle or brilliant, the orchestral writing is underpinned by a commanding grasp of form and structure by a composer who had a practical understanding of his instruments—several of which he himself played—violin, bassoon, trombone, organ, to name but four.

Tonality

Elgar's choice of F minor for the work as a whole demands consideration. During the classical and romantic periods, the key is a relatively rare one, usually reserved for emotions on the extreme side of unhappy:[128] Elgar would certainly have known Beethoven's 'Appassionata' Sonata and Tchaikovsky's Fourth Symphony, and probably Beethoven's 'Serioso' String Quartet, and Mendelssohn's last String Quartet (written as a memorial to his recently deceased sister Fanny), and his choice clearly represents his response to, and expressive intent in setting, the poem.

F minor—and the relative major, A flat, for *The Apostles* and the First Symphony—represent Elgar's most extreme flat-side keys for the opening of a major work. F minor continues to feature prominently in *The Apostles,* its opening choral melody being not entirely dissimilar to that of *The Music Makers.*

The tonality throughout is restless, so that no sooner has a key been hit upon than Elgar undermines it through rich chromaticism or modulatory activity or both. In fact, the very opening of the work with its chromatic accompaniment gives a hint of the chromatic nature of much of the work (Ex. 1a).

---

[128] Christian Friedrich Daniel Schubart, in his *Ideen zu einer Aesthetik der Tonkunst* (Vienna, 1806) described the key as expressing 'Deep depression, funereal lament, groans of misery and longing for the grave'; although Schubart's descriptions of the character of various keys can perhaps be described as idiosyncratic, there is no doubt that his views about F minor are not entirely removed from the reputation carried over the centuries for this relatively little used tonality.

This feature provides a feeling of listlessness and unease, prominent features of the work as a whole. We notice other things. The key signature of the tonic key F minor and the preponderance of minor keys—especially B flat minor, C minor, G minor—gives the music a sombre, sad, regretful nature, which expresses Elgar's mood at the time: he was unwell for much of the year with inner ear discomfort; he was especially saddened by news of the sinking of the Titanic that year;[129] and he still missed his departed friends, particularly Jaeger, to whom tribute is paid in one of the most moving passages in the entire work. There is only one prominent major key with a sharp in the key signature and that comes in stanza 4 with some extended G major (from figure 46) at the words 'till our dream shall become their present And their work in the world be done'—presenting a distinct brightening of the tonal landscape and a climactic moment at these, the most optimistic words in the poem, a feature further emphasised by the relative tonal stability of this section. Mention should also be made of the glorious C major passage at the words 'The glory about you clinging Of the glorious futures you see, Your souls with high music ringing' (from figure 92). The other point of relative tonal stability is the

---

[129] 'I have been very, very dreary and have felt this terrible Titanic disaster acutely—and have been lonely...'Letter to Alice Stuart Wortley, 17 April 1912, quoted in Jerrold Northrop Moore, *Edward Elgar The Windflower Letters: Correspondence with Alice Caroline Stuart Wortley and her Family* (Oxford University Press, 1989), p. 99. On 24 May, Elgar conducted his '*Enigma*' *Variations* at a memorial concert for the benefit of family members of the musicians who had perished in the sinking of the Titanic the month previously.

entry of the Nimrod theme with its clear modulation from E flat to A flat (from figure 51), as noted above, no doubt expressing Elgar's feelings for the 'ennobling, sober and sane' voice of his dear, departed friend (to use Elgar's own description in his Note to Ernest Newman of August 1912— as described in Chapter 1). The move to A flat also, and magnificently, prepares the way for the quotation from the Second Symphony (as noted above).

The final point at this stage about tonality concerns the unusual balance. In the first third of the work, up to around figure 38, there are frequent references to the tonic F minor. Thereafter there are only occasional references, and none at all between the Refrain, which begins stanza 8 and the final statement of the Refrain at figure 103. During this relatively long period without Refrain there is a corresponding sinking away from the tonic, which is not heard again until the very last statement of the Refrain. In short, the tonal scheme represents the opposite of the classical model, where typically the exposition expresses tonal duality, the development modulatory activity and the recapitulation tonal stability. Finally, the work ends with a note of sadness and unease, even bleakness, qualities emphasised by the quotation near the end from *Gerontius* ('Novissima hora est').

Smaller scale aspects of tonality, such as the use of modal and whole-tone scales, unusual harmonic progressions or single chords, have either been addressed under word setting or will appear at appropriate points later in this chapter.

Full Descriptive Analysis

Prelude and stanza 1. The work opens with a device found at the openings of *The Apostles, The Kingdom* and the Second

Symphony: a low tonic, in this case played by cellos, basses, bassoons and contra bassoon, third trombone, tuba and rolled kettle drum. Ritornello A, with full orchestra, is passionate, restless and notable for its chromatic accompaniment (Ex. 1a), not unlike much of the orchestral writing in Wagner's *Parsifal*.

The entry of Ritornello B (at figure 2, Ex. 1a, 1b), beginning in F minor but soon moving to the relative major, A flat, provides a remarkable transformation from agitation to calm, as unison violas and cellos, in Beethovenian manner, sing out the theme; support is provided by reduced wind and harps. The later entry of the kettle drum on a dominant pedal E flat reinforces the A flat tonality, as the *ritornello* builds up to a wonderful, agitated climax from its soft beginnings.

The first musical quotation enters at figure 6, and this is, as discussed earlier, the 'Enigma' theme in violas and cellos, followed by a seamless alternation of the 'Enigma' theme and Ritornello A, until the music fades to almost nothing.

The chorus enters at figure 10 (Ex. 2a), with the opening lines: 'We are the music makers, And we are the dreamers of dreams', in F minor, the final word 'dreams' coinciding with a short quotation from the opening of *The Dream of Gerontius* (played by strings accompanied by harps). 'Wand'ring by lone sea-breakers' coincides with the brief quotation from *Sea Pictures* (in the strings), 'And sitting by desolate streams', by the 'Enigma' quotation once more (Ex. 2a, 2b). 'World-losers and world-forsakers' is set beautifully for unaccompanied chorus in E flat minor, continuing with 'On whom the pale moon gleams', at which point a terrific crescendo on 'Yet we are the movers and shakers Of the world for ever, it seems' leads to the first huge climax on 'shakers of the world'.

Table 5.1: Complete descriptive analysis: prelude and stanza 1

Fig.	Stanza **number** and text	Description and **Quotation**	Key
		Prelude: Ritornello A	f
2		Prelude: Ritornello B	f/A flat
6		Prelude: **Enigma** theme	
10	1: Refrain: *We are the music makers,/And we are the dreamers of*		f
10.3 /11	*dreams,/* Wand'ring by lone sea-breakers,/And sitting by desolate	***Gerontius* (Judgement motive)** ***Sea Pictures***	
11.3	streams;-/World-losers and world-forsakers,/On whom the pale moon gleams:/Yet we are the movers and shakers/Of the world for ever, it seems.	**Enigma** theme **Enigma** theme	

Stanza 2. Ritornello A links the ending of stanza 1 and the beginning of stanza 2, and the *ritornello* leads into agitated

figuration (*Allegro*) and the start of stanza 2 (figure 16) and a release of massive energy as the chorus enter on 'With wonderful deathless ditties We build up the world's great cities', in C minor, followed by 'And out of a fabulous story We fashion an empire's glory', at which point the vocal parts become imitative and lead to a complex contrapuntal climax as we hear (just) a distorted phrase from 'Rule, Britannia' (in cor anglais, horns and strings), together with a snatch of 'La Marseillaise' on trumpets (B flat major, harmonised with a Neapolitan sixth), the whole passage accompanied by side drum, cymbals and bass drum, as if from a distant yet approaching imperial army.[130]

A short rendition of Ritornello A (B flat minor to B flat major) leads to 'One man with a dream' (from figure 20), where the only moving parts against the sustained chords are the harps. This sustained peaceful passage is interrupted by 'at pleasure, Shall go forth and conquer a crown', where the military characteristics return, leading to a massive climax on 'And three with a new song's measure Can trample a Kingdom down.' At this point (figure 25) all instruments (including the 'military' percussion) participate, playing as loudly as possible. The orchestral passage at this point (figure 25) features contrary motion, with the upper instruments playing simultaneously two descending, whole-tone scales (E natural, D natural, C natural, B flat, G sharp, F sharp, E natural, and, a third lower, C natural, B flat, A flat, G flat, E natural, D natural, C natural). Perhaps Elgar intended to

---

[130] These external quotations were noticed by several critics at the first performance, probably because Ernest Newman had drawn attention to them in his programme note.

suggest an exotic (biblical?) location with his unusual scale. As if to drive home the military associations of this part of the setting of O'Shaughnessy's poem, Elgar makes one final reference to 'La Marseillaise' in both brass and voices, before kettle drum, 'military' percussion, and cellos imitating drums take us to the final C minor passage of stanza 2, ending with a dominant seventh in F minor.

Table 5.2: Complete descriptive analysis: stanza 2

14.4		Ritornello A	f
16	**2**: With wonderful deathless ditties/We build up the world's great cities,/And out of a fabulous story/		c
18	We fashion an empire's glory:/	**Rule Britannia + Marseillaise.** Ritornello A	B flat b flat
20	One man with a dream, at pleasure,/Shall go forth and conquer		B flat Shifting
/24.1	a crown;/And three with a new song's measure/		/c
24.5	Can trample a kingdom down.		Whole-tone scales Long C pedal at 26

118

Stanza 3 (from figure 27). From the opening two lines, 'We, in the ages lying In the buried past of the earth', Elgar constructs four phrases of two bars each, in a chromatically descending sequence of C-B natural-B flat-A natural for unison voices and violas, whilst the upper strings have a lively, decorated version of the same sequence, with cellos in contrary motion, a deceptively simple, effective piece of word painting, suggesting both the past and a lively future. A different type of word painting appears at figure 28. For the words 'Built Nineveh with our sighing', with its biblical reference, Elgar uses the ancient Dorian mode. Here the voices are at first in unison, whilst the first violins accompany with a lively dance-like theme of one-bar's length repeated seven times. For the next biblical reference, 'And Babel itself in our mirth' Elgar has a sweeping phrase ending with a technically difficult chromatic passage in consecutive fourths for violins one and two, depicting devilish laughter.[131] The Dorian mode passage is then repeated, followed by a second rendition of the sweeping phrase and devilish laughter. For the line 'And o'erthrew them with prophesying' Elgar once more uses descending whole-tone scales (F sharp, E natural, D natural, C natural, A sharp, G sharp, and, simultaneously, D natural, C natural, B flat, A flat, F sharp, E natural). He sets the lines 'To the old of the new world's worth' and 'For each

[131] As Elgar realised when preparing the vocal score, the rapid chromatic, consecutive fourths are unplayable on the piano, hence the trouble he went to ensuring that the lower part in the right hand should be printed small, as he differentiated between large and small notes with green-ink circles; London, British Library, Add. MS. 58036.

age is a dream that is dying' simultaneously (Ex. 3), each line having its own 'subject' in a beautiful passage of double counterpoint, leading to a massive climax, ending on the dominant of F major. Over the closing bars of another rendition of Ritornello A, the Refrain is sung by choir, softly in F minor.

Table 5.3: Complete descriptive analysis: Stanza 3

27	**3**: We, in the ages lying/In the buried past of the earth,/		Shifting
28.1	Built Nineveh with our sighing,/And Babel itself in our mirth;/And o'erthrew them with prophesying/		Dorian mode Whole-tone scales
32– 36.2	To the old of the new world's worth;/For each age is a dream that is dying,/Or one that is coming to birth.	Counterpoint with two subjects (leading to massive climax)	F modulating F: V-I
36.2 37.2	Refrain: (*We are the music makers*.)	Ritornello A	b flat-f

Stanza 4 (from figure 38). The first nineteen bars of stanza 4 follow closely the contours of Ritornello B, cleverly and effectively. First violins sustain a low A flat from the F minor harmony of the conclusion of the choral Refrain, with the choir entering seven bars later on 'A breath of our inspiration', unaccompanied, with a breathtakingly effective one-bar extension of the half-diminished harmony from the equivalent point of Ritornello B, on the word 'breath'. Here, the word painting is simple yet effective, as all singers take a breath, and continue with 'of our inspiration'; the melodic line which sets these three words is then wrapped around the choral texture—sopranos, altos, tenors, in a continuation of Ritornello B, then continuing in the orchestra as the choir repeat the words, picking out harmony notes from the orchestral parts. In short, these nineteen bars form one of the loveliest passages in the entire work. From this point onwards (figure 40.6 up to figure 42) the music follows the broad contours of the equivalent point in the Prelude (figure 4 to figure 5.4), but moving in a different tonal direction, as the altos and tenors cry out magnificently 'Is the life of each generation' in A flat, repeated by other voices, followed by 'A wond'rous thing, of our dreaming.'

As noted above, the first extended filigrees in the first violins against the words 'of our dreaming' (figure 42 onwards) so call to mind concerto writing that one wonders why Elgar did not set it for solo violin. A 'wond'rous' harmonic progression at the words 'Unearthly, impossible seeming' deserves detailed description, as such subtleties can be overlooked in the glorious flow of the music. At this point (from figure 42.4, last beat), Elgar produces a series of harmonic progressions which move by semitone, and involve consecutive fifths (of the kind frowned upon by strict harmony teachers with a penchant for red ink and aversion to consecutive fifths and octaves),[132] but the effect is both exotic and remarkable, as we reach what may, deceptively, appear to be the most extreme sharp-side harmony in the entire work, with a move to the dominant of E major (but which probably represents the enharmonic equivalent of F flat), followed by C sharp minor (which probably represents the enharmonic equivalent of D flat minor) for a grand climax on the words 'The soldier, the king, and the peasant Are working together in one' (from figure 43.6, last beat). The reiteration of each vocal phrase by the orchestra drives home the climax, with added drama produced by brass playing in quavers between each glorious choral proclamation.

'Till our dreams shall become their present, And their work in the world be done' is at first presented softly before leading to a climactic *Grandioso* passage (at figure 46) with full orchestra in G major. A long G pedal, over which we hear the loveliest harmonic colourings, produces a gradual calming of atmosphere and dynamic level and brightening of tonal landscape, so that by the time we reach figure 48.9, there is a sense of natural ending for this part of the Ode combined with scene setting for the next stanza with contralto soloist. Only the violas and harp are left at the end, playing G, B, D, changing to B flat at the last moment.

---

[132] The use of parallel fifths at this point could have been suggested by the section 'Des Helden Widersacher' ('The Hero's Adversaries') in Strauss's *Ein Heldenleben*.

Table 5.4: Complete descriptive analysis: Stanza 4

38		Ritornello B	f/A flat
38.6	**4**: A breath of our Inspiration/Is the life of each generation:/A wond'rous thing of our dreaming/Unearthly, impossible seeming-		E flat Modulating
/43.6	/The soldier, the king, and the peasant/Are working together in one,/Till our dream shall become their present,/And their	(Climactic)	/c sharp Modulating
/46	work in the world be done.		/G (G pedal)

Stanza 5 (from figure 49.1). That change of note from B natural to B flat was significant, as it prepares for the opening contralto solo in G minor (Ex. 4a). Here the words are 'They had no vision amazing Of the goodly house they are raising.' Elgar indicates that the style is *quasi recitativo*, and this quality merges into a melodic line based on Ritornello B, for the words 'They had no divine foreshowing Of the land to which they are going', modulating magnificently to E flat for the opening of the Nimrod passage (Ex. 4b) which merges into the A flat quotation from the Second Symphony, as described in some detail above. The text at this point is 'But

on one man's soul it hath broken, A light that doth not depart;
And his look, or a word he hath spoken, Wrought flame in
another man's heart'.

Table 5.5: Complete descriptive analysis: Stanza 5

49.1	**5**: They had no vision amazing/Of the goodly house they are raising;/They had no divine foreshowing/Of the land to which they are going:/	Contralto solo, quasi recit. Vocal line based on Ritornello B	g modulating
51	But on one man's soul it hath broken,/A light that doth not depart;/	Contralto solo with chorus; **'Nimrod'**	E flat-A flat
53	And his look, or a word he hath spoken,/Wrought flame in another man's heart.	(End of) **Second Symphony**	A flat

Stanza 6 (from figure 55) is the only stanza without a
musical quotation and the point at which the word setting
becomes flexible, with interruptions, repeats and text-
overlaps between different voices, a process which intensifies
from here until the end of the work. The opening words, 'And
therefore today is thrilling With a past day's late fulfilling' are

set in B flat minor with an energetic string accompaniment (perhaps recalling the orchestral rhythms in 'Tuba mirum' from Verdi's *Requiem*). At the repetition of these words, Elgar unleashes an orchestral melody with chromatic bass (figure 55.4) which is by turns striking and passionate, before a return to the energetic accompaniment and repeat of the passionate melody, eventually leading to an astonishing (even after repeated hearings) Refrain of 'We are the music makers, And we are the dreamers of dreams' in B flat minor and marked to be sung and played as loudly as possible, subsiding for a return of the energetic rhythm. 'And the multitudes are enlisted In the faith that their fathers resisted...And bringing to pass, as they may, In the world, for its joy or its sorrow, The dream that was scorned yesterday', leads to another very loud Refrain, this time of the words 'We are the movers and shakers Of the world for ever, it seems'. At figure 65, with the words 'The multitudes are bringing to pass the dream', a rich contrapuntal passage ensues, during which the choral parts leap up by a minor seventh onto an *appoggiatura/portamento*, the ultimate in emotional expression. After a return of the orchestral melody with chromatic bass, the expressive intensity subsides as the harmony lands firmly on C (as the dominant of F minor) for another statement of Ritornello A. Stanza 6 ends with those wonderful parallel fifths heard earlier in stanza 4.

Table 5.6: Complete descriptive analysis: Stanza 6

55	**6**: And therefore to-day is thrilling/With a past day's late fulfilling;/And the multitudes are enlisted/In thc faith that their fathers resisted/And, scorning the dream of to-morrow,/Are bringing to pass, as they may,/In the world, for its joy or its sorrow,/The dream that was scorned yesterday.	Contralto solo with chorus	b flat Shifting
60	Refrain: (*We are the music makers…*)	Refrain (at the end of a massive climax)	b flat
61	(Resumption of 6) And therefore today is thrilling…		Shifting
64.7–65	Refrain: (*We are the movers and shakers…*)	(Climactic)	Shifting
67.7		Ritornello A	f (over dom. pedal)

Stanza 7 (from figure 70.5). The opening of stanza 7 overlaps with the end of the orchestral passage which concluded stanza 6, but now in A flat. After a pause on 'But we' the ensuing lines 'With our dreaming and singing, Ceaseless and sorrowless we! The glory about us clinging Of the glorious futures we see, Our souls with high music ringing' are set to the double counterpoint heard earlier in stanza 3 (from figure 32), but at a slower tempo and softer dynamic. At the end of the words 'Of the glorious futures we see', continuing with 'Oh men! It must ever be That we dwell in our dreaming and our singing', there is an extended quotation of the Enigma theme in the woodwind (in E flat minor over a dominant pedal) which quotation is joined by three more: passages from the Violin Concerto first and second movements (in the strings) and figuration from *The Apostles* in the woodwind (in F major). This part of the Ode ends with B flat major dominant harmony and a silent pause.

Table 5.7: Complete descriptive analysis: Stanza 7

70.5	**7**: But we, with our dreaming and singing,/Cease-less and sorrowless we!/The glory about us clinging/	Counterpoint with two subjects (reprised from fig. 32, but softer and gentler pace)	A flat
74.4…75	Of the glorious futures we see,/Our souls with high music ringing:/Oh men! It must ever be/That we dwell,	…'**Enigma**' theme	…e flat (over dom. pedal)
76/77.5	in our dreaming and our singing,/A little apart from ye.	/**Violin Concerto (I and II)**, '**Enigma**' theme and ***The Apostles***	e flat/E flat… F

Stanza 8 (from figure 78). The F major chord's fifth degree (note C) which ended the seventh stanza resoles onto F minor and music of the Refrain to the words, 'For we are afar with the dawning And the suns that are not yet high'. It is easy to overlook the deceptively simple harmonic procedure which Elgar employs to achieve another glorious effect in this passage, but study of it reveals yet another example of scene setting, this time within a short space of time. The harmonies are as follows:

Figure 78 and 78.1: F minor: i to v (with flattened leading note)
Figure 78.2: iv6/4 and i5/3
Figure 78.3: iv and i6/3
Figure 78.4: B flat minor: iv6/4
Figure 78.5: unison B flat notes

Each of the choral homophonic statements is overlapped by portentous rapid scalic passages. Everything points to a continuation in B flat minor, but—in the manner of the great classical or classic/romantic composers Haydn, Mozart, Beethoven and Brahms—Elgar confounds expectation, here with a magnificent resolution into B flat major (figure 79), as *a cappella* homophonic chorus express the words 'And out of the infinite morning Intrepid you hear us cry' with a whisper that grows into a cry of victory to the motto theme of the First Symphony, made all the more spine-tingling by being sung at first rather than played, and continuing climactically until figure 81. The First Symphony quotation reaches a choral climax, being a tone higher than in the Symphony, at figure 80.7 as sopranos reach up to top B flat on the word 'cry'. Reference to the Almighty is made for the first time around this point: 'How, spite of your human scorning, Once more God's future draws nigh', as, over a pedal note in E flat minor, triplets in the brass, kettle drum and bass drum lend a decidedly military sound. The ensuing Ritornello A is given a frantic element by the addition of a semiquaver accompaniment in trombones wind and lower strings, as mentioned earlier (figure 82 onwards), as the words turn from victory to warning: 'And already goes forth the warning That ye of the past must die'. Here we have another appearance of the whole-tone scale first heard towards the end of stanza 2, now given a funereal quality with the kettle drum, played at this point 'with drum stick', and bass drum. The stanza ends with three bars of closing material in the lower strings, the first violas having the plaintive, C minor melody.

Table 5.8: Complete descriptive analysis: Stanza 8

78	**8**: For we are afar with the dawning/And the suns that are not yet high,/	(Varied) Refrain	f
78.4…79	And out of the infinite morning/Intrepid you hear us cry-/How, spite of your human scorning,/Once more God's future draws nigh,/	**…First Symphony** (motto) (Climactic)	B flat
82		Ritornello A	c
82.1	And already goes forth the warning/That ye of the past must die.	Whole-tone scale on 'die'. Long C pedal	c

Stanza 9 (from figure 85). Elgar's first thought, according to a sketch,[133] had been to begin this section with a unison E flat, beginning softly with a *crescendo* to *f*—in similar manner to the very opening of the Ode—but he subsequently did away with the bar of unison and entered with the two and a half bars of agitated string writing punctuated with wind, before the soloist enters with a glorious octave leap, the visceral quality of which is enhanced by the *portamento* (as used earlier, for example at figure 65) to the upper octave, with 'Great hail! we cry to the comers From the dazzling unknown shore'. At this point, Ritornello B enters for an extended passage, as the soloist sings the words 'Bring us hither your sun and your summers, And renew our world as of yore; You shall teach us your song's new numbers, And things that we dreamed not before: Bring us hither your sun and your summers, Ceaseless and sorrowless ye'. Sometimes the voice doubles the Ritornello B melody, at other times it sings a countermelody, sings in imitation, or otherwise caresses the melody in an extended period, as the tonality moves around B flat minor and D flat major.

At figure 92, and the words from stanza 7, 'The glory about you clinging Of the glorious futures you see', the tonality changes gloriously to C major with chromatic colouring, over a dominant pedal, with the harmonic tension rising so much as to demand resolution, which appears in climactic fashion with chord I of C major at the words 'Your souls with high music ringing', followed by four bars of simple, diatonic harmony before a move to A minor at figure

---

[133] London, British Library, Add. MS. 63159, f. 59.

92.19, as the chorus enter with 'Oh men! it must ever be That we dwell, in our dreaming and singing, A little apart from ye', with another statement of Ritornello B, at a climactic point at which the soloist re-enters (at figure 95), overlapping the chorus, with a resumption of stanza 9:'You shall teach us your song's new numbers, And things that we dreamed not before', as the tonality moves from C minor to A flat. Here, the word setting is at its most flexible, as soloist and chorus sing different lines of text simultaneously in a manner reminiscent of the closing passages of Beethoven's Ninth Symphony (as described above).

At figure 97, Elgar repeats the idea from figure 92, but the key is now D flat with chromatic colouring over a dominant pedal, for the words (from stanza 8) 'For we are afar with the dawning', as the soloist overlaps with words from stanza 9, 'And renew our world as of yore'. The resolution in D flat is more extensive than in the earlier passage, and the overlap between soloist and chorus, the two elements with different words, provides a more intense climax to the passage around figure 92, especially with the effective participation of horns and trombones.

Ritornello B returns at figure 99, as the music fades to almost nothing on the soloist's words 'And things that we dreamed not before' with the final syllable supported only by F and D flat in divided first violins. At figure 100, the soloist continues with 'Yea' (long pause), 'in spite of a dreamer who slumbers, And a singer who sings no more', accompanied by those parallel fifths which we heard earlier (at figures 43.4 following and 70 following). The glorious cadence between figures 100.6 and 101 is similar to the one between 43.5 and 43.7, both involving an interrupted cadence, but whereas the earlier instance exploded into 'The soldier, the king, and the peasant' this one moves extremely softly to the final quotation acknowledged by Elgar—'Novissima hora est' from *Gerontius*—as the words 'a singer who sings no more' are repeated against Ritornello A, until a repeat of 'Novissima hora est', transposed from F sharp minor to B minor, before the final statement of Ritornello A in E minor, fading to almost nothing, and pausing on a single note E natural.

The E natural is the leading note of F minor, the key of the Ode as a whole, yet there is no sense in which the tonic key has been prepared for its final expression. Instead, the musical atmosphere is one of sorrow in the wilderness, made more so by the remoteness of the tonal landscape at this point. After a long pause, Elgar introduces what could be described as a 'borrowing' or 'quotation' (unacknowledged by the composer), at the start of the final phrase.

This final phrase (from figure 100, Ex. 5) is perhaps the most curious of all. It begins with a half-diminished chord (played by woodwind and strings): a minor third, diminished fifth and minor seventh above the bass note G. Although half-diminished sevenths are a regular part of Elgar's harmonic resource, both in earlier works and in this one (the lovely example at figure 39 having already been commented on), the way in which this chord is stated here in isolation at first, and without context—taking up a whole bar with nothing else— is what makes it so remarkable. Although at different pitches, it is basically the same as the famous chord from the opening of Wagner's opera *Tristan und Isolde*—the so-called 'Tristan chord'.[134] Elgar seems to have almost stumbled on the idea, for a sketch shows the chord as part of a sequence and placed against the first notes of the final choral entry;[135] even after he has isolated the chord, he goes on adding refinements, for in a printer's proof of the vocal score we find an added dynamic refinement: *ppp* is changed to *fppp* (in Elgar's hand) for extra emphasis.[136] We cannot even be certain that Elgar recognised the chord as a 'borrowing' from Wagner, or that he was consciously quoting it—surprising though it would be if such a knowledgeable, sensitive musician was unaware of the link between such a conspicuous sound and the German

---

[134] The famous chord which occurs at the opening of Wagner's opera *Tristan und Isolde*, the very first chord, consists of the following intervals: augmented fourth, augmented sixth, augmented ninth against the bass note F, and is enharmonically equivalent to a half-diminished chord (F-A flat-C flat-E flat), but is susceptible to various descriptions and interpretations (as evidenced by the extensive literature on the subject). Wagner used the chord as part of a phrase ending with a dominant seventh of A minor. Although the chord was not 'invented' by Wagner, it is often referred to as the 'Tristan chord' because of the characteristic use of it in that opera. The phrase, or part of it, containing the chord has been quoted in several works after Wagner, including by Debussy, who uses it satirically and famously in the *Children's Corner* (1908), and Alban Berg in the last movement of the *Lyric Suite* (1926). I am grateful to Julian Rushton for help with this description (in an email, 18 November 2022).

[135] London, British Library, Add. MS. 63153, f. 58 (59).

[136] London, British Library, MS. Mus. 1843 (M66), eighth bundle of printers-proofs.

composer's opera.[137] Whatever the answer, the chord as used by Wagner acted as part of a *Leitmotiv*, probably for unresolved longing, and here in *The Music Makers* it seems to express desolation, in a way which, as discussed earlier, was hardly justified by O'Shaughnessy's words, which combine sadness with optimism. Although the chord appears at first unannounced and unprepared, the inner harmony note F provides the note for the ensuing choral entry, as the orchestra continues with the phrase, thereby connecting the 'Tristan chord' with the complete sentence in a manner which is both surprising and effective.

Bringing back the Refrain one last time, as if the end of a dream, was Elgar's final stroke of genius—'We are the music makers, And we are the dreamers of dreams'—thereby presenting an unambiguous unity to the work as a whole, but the Ode ends in desolation with a very low F minor triad played by violas, cellos, double basses and kettle drum, leaving double basses alone with octave F: literally the depths of orchestral sound, and expressively the depths of sorrow, as the music makers disappear.

---

[137] Elgar saw *Tristan und Isolde* for the first time on 29 July 1892 at Bayreuth, an experience for which he had prepared himself by studying a printed analysis; he acquired a vocal score of the opera on 1 June 1893—see Moore, *Edward Elgar: A Creative Life*, pp. 164, 172–173—and had a good knowledge of the opera's *Leitmotiven*, as he demonstrated when enthusing to Rosa Burley about *Tristan*; see Rosa Burley and Frank C. Carruthers, *Edward Elgar: The Record of a Friendship* (London: Barrie and Jenkins, 1972), pp. 56–58.

Table 5.9: Complete descriptive analysis: Stanza 9

85	**9**: Great hail! we cry to the comers/From the dazzling unknown shore;/	Contralto solo	c shifting
88	Bring us hither your sun and your summers,/And renew our world as of yore; (Text from 7 interspersed in a fluid manner)	Contralto solo. Ritornell B	b flat/D flat
92	(**7**) Your glory about you...Your souls...	Contralto solo with chorus	C: V-I
95	**9** (continued): You shall teach us your song's new numbers,/And things that we dreamed not before:/	Contralto solo with chorus. Ritornello B	c-A flat-shifting
100	**9** (concluded): Yea, in spite of	Contralto solo with chorus	Shifting

	a dreamer who slumbers,/		
101	And a singer who sings no more.	*Gerontius* (**'Novissima hora est'**)	Shifting - b
102.3		Ritornello A, ending with single note E	e
103	Refrain: (*We are the music makers,/And we are the dreamers of dreams.*)	Chorus with orchestra: Refrain	'Tristan chord' - f

Summary

At the heart of this book lie three hypotheses, the third one of which is that Elgar's setting represents a more innovatory artistic creation than is usually recognised. The main innovation is the way in which he incorporates musical quotations, most from Elgar's own music but two from acknowledged external sources, the precise handling of which must count as unique despite historical precedents in terms of borrowed material.

To achieve this successfully, Elgar needed to provide structure and coherence to his musical scheme. This he did in various ways: by a key scheme beginning and ending in F minor with recurring references to it, but which allows for a highly personal interpretation of O'Shaughnessy's text; by the use of refrains (a method entirely absent from O'Shaughnessy's poem); by the use of recurring motives, especially the two *ritornelli*; and by the varied repetition of

137

certain passages, in particular, the counterpoint with two subjects (occurring, symmetrically, the first time about a third of the way through, and the second time about two thirds of the way through).

Chapter 5
Conclusions
Reading Beyond the Notes

Despite Elgar's limited debt to Strauss's *Ein Heldenleben*, *The Music Makers* is decidedly and impressively innovative, especially in the way in which it goes beyond any other works for choir and orchestra in successfully incorporating material 'borrowed', both from Elgar's own works and external sources. Many of the early newspaper critics appreciated the success of this novelty, but a few, especially from *The Telegraph* and *The Times*, did not, a fact which may have upset the deeply sensitive composer. It is a further contention of this study that *The Music Makers*, despite its chequered reputation and fluctuating status, should take its place alongside *Gerontius*, *The Apostles* and *The Kingdom* as one of the composer's most expressive and convincing works, despite its smaller scale and very different style.

Elgar's Ode has suffered especially from negative responses to the poetry which he set. However, as this guide has endeavoured to show, placing O'Shaughnessy's Ode in cultural and aesthetic context helps our understanding of the strengths of its form and expression. Further, placing aspects of the poet's biography against the composer's—in that both O'Shaughnessy and Elgar suffered an inferiority complex arising from their relatively humble backgrounds and limited education, handicaps against which their achievements were all the more impressive—helps in our understanding of Elgar's attraction to, and sympathy with, both the poet and his poetry.

Although Elgar's initial impetus for *The Music Makers* was the suitability of O'Shaughnessy's poem—crying out to be set to music, and therefore an attractive vehicle for an elaborate setting likely to attract a commission from a music festival such as Leeds, or, as it turned out, Birmingham—as the composer worked intensively he can hardly have failed to be aware of the element of manifesto in both the poem and his setting. The crucial importance of music and musicians in the history of civilisation, the constant evolution and re-birth of the art form, and its neglect at our peril, are themes which sing through the words and music. O'Shaughnessy's profound interest in music, his earnest desire to bring musical qualities to his verse, Elgar's profound interest in literature, his earnest belief in the need to constantly renew through the efforts of new generations of musicians (as expressed in his Birmingham University lectures): these elements come together in the most apposite, united artistic form.

Furthermore, although this may not have been Elgar's initial aim, *The Music Makers* expresses strong autobiographical elements. The musical quotations were selected because of their appropriateness for the words at any point, but in the process the composer inevitably reviews his creative life, at least over the past twelve or so years, the earliest of the 'self-borrowed' music dating from 1899 (the

140

'*Enigma' Variations* and *Sea Pictures*) and the latest from 1911 (the Second Symphony). The mood of the *Variations* theme, expressing that sadness and loneliness which he so often felt but accepted as an essential element in the career of the composer, the depths of sadness in the *Gerontius* quotations, the stability and nobility of the 'Nimrod' passage, representing his profound feelings of admiration for, and gratitude to, August Jaeger, the rousing confidence of the First Symphony quotation contrasting with the deep yearning of the Second Symphony reference, and the profound symbolism of the Violin Concerto quotations: all these elements add up to a most remarkable autobiographical artistic expression. Not for nothing did Elgar declare to Alice Stuart Wortley: 'I have written out my soul in the Concerto, Sym II and the Ode and you know it and my vitality seems in them now and I am happy it is so—in those three works I have *shewn* myself.'[138]

The Music Makers can similarly be read as a metaphor for the triumphs and trials of Elgar's career thus far. The joyous, rapturous passages perhaps symbolising the hard-won victories—particularly the *'Enigma' Variations*, the First Symphony and the Violin Concerto—but the prevailingly sad passages, especially the ending, his feelings of failure: the disastrous first performance of *Gerontius*, the muted initial reaction to his Second Symphony, and so on. It is even possible to read into the prevailing sadness and gloom of the

---

[138] Elgar to Alice Stuart Wortley, 29 August 1912, as quoted in Jerrold Northrop Moore, *The Windflower Letters: Correspondence with Alice Stuart Wortley and her Family* (Oxford University Press, 1989), p. 107.

ending a metaphor for the world on the edge of a precipice, but that would be with the benefit of historical hindsight— although (as described in Chapter 2) the European tensions and fears connected with the Balkan conflict may well have had some bearing on the negative attitude of some critics in 1912 to O'Shaughnessy's verse of 1874.

Elgar was keen to emphasise that the work could be appreciated even by listeners who recognise none of the quotations. Most of the music is originally composed: the 'borrowed' themes are in most cases heard briefly against 'new' music. Even the extended 'Nimrod' passage, the orchestral writing of which is at first virtually unchanged from the op. 36 masterpiece, places the contralto soloist's line in variation to it, and the modulation around the point of the choral re-entry and subsequent merging with music from the First Symphony probably represent one of the composer's most sublime inspirations. Structurally, the piece is strong, with *ritornelli* and refrains forming unifying elements and the tonal scheme acting both structurally and expressively, even though the organisation of keys is unusual.

The time has surely come when we need no longer defend *The Music Makers*; instead, we may wish to celebrate one of Elgar's most singular achievements.

Appendix 1

'Ode'
Arthur O'Shaughnessy (from *Music and Moonlight*)

We are the music makers,
And we are the dreamers of dreams,
Wandering by lone sea-breakers,
And sitting by desolate streams;-
World-losers and world-forsakers
On whom the pale moon gleams:
Yet we are the movers and shakers
Of the world for ever, it seems.

With wonderful deathless ditties
We build up the world's great cities,
And out of a fabulous story
We fashion an empire's glory:
One man with a dream, at pleasure,
Shall go forth and conquer a crown;
And three with a new song's measure
Can trample a kingdom down.

We, in the ages lying
In the buried past of the earth,
Built Nineveh with our sighing,
And Babel itself in our mirth;
And o'erthrew them with prophesying
To the old of the new world's worth;
For each age is a dream that is dying,
Or one that is coming to birth.

A breath of our inspiration
Is the life of each generation;
A wondrous thing of our dreaming
Unearthly, impossible seeming—
The soldier, the king, and the peasant
Are working together in one,
Till our dream shall become their present,
And their work in the world be done.

They had no vision amazing
Of the goodly house they are raising;
They had no divine foreshowing
Of the land to which they are going:
But on one man's soul it hath broken,
A light that doth not depart;
And his look, or a word he hath spoken,
Wrought flame in another man's heart.

And therefore to-day is thrilling
With a past day's late fulfilling;
And the multitudes are enlisted
In the faith that their fathers resisted

And, scorning the dream of to-morrow,
Are bringing to pass, as they may,
In the world, for its joy or its sorrow,
The dream that was scorned yesterday.

But we, with our dreaming and singing,
Ceaseless and sorrowless we!
The glory about us clinging
Of the glorious futures we see,
Our souls with high music ringing:
O men! It must ever be
That we dwell, in our dreaming and singing,
A little apart from ye.

For we are afar with the dawning
And the suns that are not yet high,
And out of the infinite morning
Intrepid you hear us cry—
How, spite of your human scorning,
Once more God's future draws nigh,
And already goes forth the warning
That ye of the past must die.

Great hail! we cry to the comers
From the dazzling unknown shore;
Bring us hither your sun and summers,
And renew our world as of yore;
You shall teach us your song's new numbers,
And things that we dreamed not before:
Yea, in spite of a dreamer who slumbers,
And a singer who sings no more.

Appendix 2

Early Performances of *The Music Makers*

Date	Venue and Occasion	Performers	Reviews
1 October 1912 (world premiere)	Town Hall, Birmingham; Birmingham Festival	Festival Chorus, Birmingham Musical Festival Orchestra, Muriel Foster (contralto), Sir Edward Elgar (conductor)	*Birmingham Gazette*; *The Daily News and Leader; The Daily Post*; *The Daily Telegraph*; *The Morning Post*; *The Times*; *The Yorkshire Post*; all 2 October; unidentified newspaper; *Christian Science Monitor*, Boston, MA, 5 (?) October; *The Musical Times*, November
13 November 1912	The Dome, Brighton; Brighton Festival	Brighton Municipal Choir and Orchestra, Muriel Foster	*The Morning Post*, 14 November; *The Musical Times,* December; *The*

		(contralto), Sir Edward Elgar (conductor)	*Sunday Times*, 17 November; unidentified newspaper
19 November 1912	Public Hall, Worcester	Worcester Festival Chorus, Sara Silvers (contralto), Ivor Atkins (conductor)	Unidentified newspaper
21 November 1912	Victoria Hall, Sunderland	Sunderland Philharmonic Society, Leeds Symphony Orchestra, Lucy Nuttall (contralto), Nicholas Kilburn (conductor)	*Sunderland Echo*, 22 November
28 November 1912	Royal Albert Hall, London	Royal Choral Society, Muriel Foster (contralto), Sir Frederick Bridge (conductor)	*The Morning Post*; *The Times*; both 29 November; *The Christian Science Monitor*; unidentified newspaper; *Zeitschrift der internationalen Musikgesell-schaft*, 14/3 (December 1912), 78–80 (Charles Maclean)

November 1912	Exmouth	Exmouth Choral Society, Alice Larking (contralto), Raymond Wilmot (conductor)	Unidentified newspaper
30 November 1912	Victoria Rooms, Bristol	Bristol New Philharmonic Society, Phyllis Lett (contralto), Arnold Barter (conductor)	*Bristol Times and Mirror*, 1 December
18 February 1913	Philharmonic Hall, Liverpool	Worcester Festival Chorus, Phyllis Lett (contralto), Frederic Cowen (conductor)	*Liverpool Courier*, *Liverpool Daily Post*, 19 February
January or February 1913	Excelsior Hall, Bethnal Green, London	Oxford House Choral Society, Norah Dawnay (contralto), Cuthbert Kelly (conductor)	*The Daily Telegraph*, 4 March
3 March 1913	Queen's Hall, London	Oxford House Choral Society,	*The Daily Telegraph*, 4 March

		Norah Dawnay (contralto), Cuthbert Kelly (conductor)	
March 1913	Town Hall, Bishop Auckland	Bishop Auckland Musical Society, Lady Maud Warrender (contralto), Nicholas Kilburn (conductor)	*The Yorkshire Post*
16 April 1913	Carnegie Hall, New York	Columbia University Festival Chorus, Mildred Potter (contralto), Walter Henry Hall (conductor)	*The New York Times*, 17 April; 2 unidentified newspapers

Appendix 3

A Listener's Analytical Guide to Elgar's *The Music Makers*

Figure	Stanza **Number** and Text	Description **Quotation**	Key
		Prelude: Ritornello A	f
2		Prelude: Ritornello B	f/A flat
6		Prelude: **Enigma** theme	Modulating
10	**1**: Refrain: *We are the music makers,/And we are the dreamers of*	Chorus	f
10.3	*dreams/*	***Gerontius* ('Judgement' Motive)**	
11	Wandering by lone		
/11.3	seabreakers,/ And sitting by desolate	***Sea Pictures***	

	streams;- /World-losers and world-forsakers,/On whom the pale moon gleams:/Yet we are the movers and shakers/Of the world for ever, it seems.	**Enigma** theme

Enigma theme | |
| 14.4 | | Ritornello A | f |
| 16 | **2**: With wonderful deathless ditties/We build up the world's great cities,/And out of a fabulous story/ | | c |
| 18 | We fashion an empire's glory:/ | **Rule Britannia** +

Marseillaise...

Ritornello A | B flat

b flat |
20	One man with a dream, at pleasure,/Shall go forth and conquer a		B flat Shifting
/24.1	crown;/And three with a new song's measure/		/c
24.5	Can trample a kingdom down.	**Marseillaise**	Whole-tone scales Long

			C pedal at 26
27	**3**: We, in the ages lying/In the buried past of the earth,/		Shifting
28.1	Built Nineveh with our sighing,/And Babel itself in our mirth;/And o'erthrew them with prophesying/		Dorian mode Whole-tone scales
32–36.2	To the old of the new world's worth;/For each age is a dream that is dying,/Or one that is coming to birth.	Counterpoint with two subjects (leading to massive climax)	F modulating F: V-I
36.2 37.1	Refrain: (*We are the music makers...*)	Ritornello A	b flat - f
38 38.6	**4**: A breath of our inspiration/Is the life of each generation;/A wondrous thing of our	Ritornello B	f/A flat E flat Modulating

/43.6	dreaming/ Unearthly Impossible seeming-/The soldier, the king, and the peasant/Are working together in one,/Till our dream shall become their present,/And their work in the world be done.	(Climactic)	/c sharp Modulating /G (G pedal)
45			
46			
49.1	**5**: They had no vision amazing/Of the goodly house they are raising;/They had no divine foreshowing/Of the land to which they are going:/	Contralto solo, quasi recitative. /Vocal line based on Ritornello B	g modulating
51	But on one man's soul it hath broken,/A light that doth not depart;/	Contralto solo with chorus; **'Nimrod'**	E flat-A flat

53 And his look, or a word he hath spoken,/Wrought flame in another man's heart.		(End of) **Second Symphony**	A flat
55	**6**: And therefore to-day is thrilling/ With a past day's late fulfilling;/ And the multitudes are enlisted/In the faith that their fathers resisted/And, scorning the dream of tomorrow,/Are bringing to pass, as they may,/In the world, for its joy or its sorrow,/The dream that was scorned yesterday.	Contralto solo with chorus	b flat Shifting
60	Refrain: (*We are the music makers…*)	Refrain (at the end of a massive climax)	b flat
61	(Resumption of 6) And therefore		Shifting

	today is thrilling…		
64.7–65	Refrain: (*We are the movers and shakers…*)	(Climactic)	Shifting to E flat
67.7		Ritornello A	f (over dom. pedal)
70.5	**7**: But we, with our dreaming and singing,/ Ceaseless and sorrowless we!/The glory about us clinging/	Counterpoint with two subjects (reprised from fig. 32, but softer and gentler pace)	A flat
74.4…75	Of the glorious futures we see,/Our souls with high music ringing:/ 'Oh men! It must ever be/That we dwell',	**'Enigma'** theme	…e flat (over dom. pedal)
76/77.5	in our dreaming and our singing,/A little apart from ye.	**/Violin Concerto** (I and II), and **'Enigma'** theme and ***The Apostles***	e flat/E flat F

78	**8**: For we are afar with the dawning/ And the suns that are not yet high,/	(Varied) Refrain	f
78.4.79	And out of the infinite morning/ Intrepid you hear us cry-/How, spite of your human scorning,/ Once more God's future draws nigh,/	**First Symphony** (motto) (Climactic)	B flat
82		Ritornello A	c
82.1	And already goes forth the warning/That ye of the past must die.	Whole-tone scale on 'die'.	c Long C pedal
85	**9**: Great hail! we cry to the comers/From the dazzling unknown shore;/	Contralto solo	c shifting
88	Bring us hither your sun and your summers,/ And renew our world as of	Contralto solo. Ritornello B	b flat/D flat

	yore; (Text from 7 interspersed in a fluid manner)		
92	(7) The glory about…Your souls…	Contralto solo with chorus	C: V-I
		Ritornello B	a/C
95	9 (continued) You shall teach us your song's new numbers,/And things that we dreamed not before:/	Contralto solo with chorus. Ritornello B	c-A flat
100	9 (concluded). Yea, in spite of a dreamer who slumbers,/	Contralto solo with chorus	Shifting
101	And a singer who sings no more.	**Gerontius ('Novissima hora est')**	Shifting—b
102.3		Ritornello A, ending with single note E	e
103	Refrain: (*We are the music makers,/And we are the dreamers of dreams.*)	Chorus with orchestra: Refrain	'Tristan chord'—f

Appendix 4

Musical Examples from *The Music Makers*

Ex. 1a, opening to fig. 2.1

Ex. 1b, from fig. 2.2 to fig. 5.4

Ex. 2a, from fig. 10 to fig. 11

Ex, 2b, from figure 11.1 to fig. 12.1

Ex. 3, from fig. 32 to fig. 32.5

Ex. 4a, from 49 to fig. 50.8

Ex. 4b, from fig. 50.9 to fig. 52.3

Ex. 5, from fig. 103 to the end

THE MUSIC MAKERS.

A. O'Shaughnessy.

Edward Elgar, Op. 69.

Example 1a

Example 1b

Example 2a

Example 2b

26

Example 3

Example 4a

Example 4b

Example 5

Bibliography

Primary Sources

Elgar's Sketches for *The Music Makers*:
London, British Library, Add. MS. 47902, Add. MS. 47908, Add. MS. 58000, Add. MS. 58001, Add. MS. 58002, Add. MS. 63153, Add. MS. 63154, Add. MS. 63156, Add. MS. 63158, Add. MS. 63159, Add. MS. 63160, Add. MS. 63161, Add. MS. 63162, MS. Mus. 1843/1/6, MS. Mus. 1843 (M66).

Autograph Vocal Score of *The Music Makers*:
London, British Library, Add. MS. 58036.

Printer's proof-sheets of the Vocal Score of *The Music Makers*:
London, British Museum, MS. Mus. 1843/2.

Autograph Full Score of *The Music Makers*:
Birmingham, Cadbury Research Library, University of Birmingham, EE 3/6.

Newspaper Reviews of Early Performances of *The Music Makers:*

Bristol Times and Mirror, 1 December 1912.

Liverpool Courier, 19 February 1913.

Liverpool Daily Post, 19 February 1913.

Sunderland Echo, 22 November 1912.

The Birmingham Gazette, 2 October 1912.

The Christian Science Monitor (Boston, Mass.), 5 (?) October 1912, 29 November 1912.

The Daily News and Leader, 2 October 1912.

The Daily Post, 2 October 1912.

The Daily Telegraph, 2 October 1912, 4 March 1913.

The Morning Post, 2 October 1912, 14 November 1912, 29 November 1912.

The New York Times, 17 April 1913.

The Sunday Times, 17 November 1912.

The Times, 2 October 1912, 29 November 1912.

The Yorkshire Post, 2 October 1912, March 1913.

Newspaper Articles:

The Daily News, 25 March 1904 (article by Edward Baughan).

The Daily Telegraph, 6 January 1912 (article by Robin Legge).

Collected Poems of Arthur O'Shaughnessy:

An Epic of Women and Other Poems. London: John Camden Hotten, 1870.

Lays of France (Founded on the Lays of Marie), 2nd edition. London: Chatto and Windus, 1874.

Music and Moonlight: Poems and Songs. London: Chatto and Windus, 1874.

Songs of a Worker. London: Chatto and Windus, 1881.

Other Sources

Anderson, Robert and Moore, Jerrold Northrop (eds.). *The Music Makers, The Spirit of England, With Proud Thanksgiving*, Elgar Compete Edition, vol. 10. Sevenoaks, Novello, 1986.

———*Symphony No. 2*: Op. 63, Elgar Complete Edition. Sevenoaks: Novello, 1984.

———*Variations on an Original Theme for Orchestra*: Op. 36, Elgar Complete Edition. Sevenoaks: Novello, 1986.

Bird, Martin (ed.). *Edward Elgar: Collected Correspondence* (Elgar Works), V/1 (2013), *Provincial Musician: Diaries 1857–1896,* V/2 (2015), *Road to Recognition: Diaries 1897–1901*, V/3 (2016), *The Path to Knighthood: Diaries 1902–1904* (2016).

Bird, Martin. 'Reactions to *The Music Makers'*, *The Elgar Society Journal*, 17/6 (2012), 13–15.

Buckley, Robert, J. *Sir Edward Elgar.* London: John Lane: The Bodley Head, 1905.

Burley, Rosa and Carruthers, Frank. *Edward Elgar: The Record of a Friendship.* London: Barrie and Jenkins, 1972.

Csizmadia, Florian. *Leitmotivik und verwandte Techniken in den Chorwerken von Edward Elgar: Analysen und Kontexte.* Berlin: Verlag Dr Köster, 2017.

Dunhill, Thomas, F. *Sir Edward Elgar.* London and Glasgow: Blackie, 1938.

Gosse, Edmund. 'Obituary: Arthur O'Shaughnessy', in *The Academy*, 457 (5 February 1881).

———*Silhouettes.* London: Heinemann, 1925.

Harper-Scott, J.P.E. *Elgar: An Extraordinary Life.* London: The Associated Board of the Royal Schools of Music, 2007.

Hodgkins, Geoffrey. 'E's Favourite Picture: Elgar and the Pre-Raphaelites', in *The Victorian Web: Literature, History & Culture in the Age of Victoria* (2007), https://victorianweb.org/mt/elgar/1.htm.

Howes, Frank. 'The Two Elgars', in *Music and Letters*, February 1935, 26–29.

Hunt, Donald. 'Thoughts on *The Music Makers*: A Conductor's Viewpoint', in *The Elgar Society*, 17/6, (1912), 4–12.

———*Elgar and the Three Choirs Festival.* Worcester: Osborne, 1999.

Jaeger, A.J. *Analytical Notes to* The Dream of Gerontius, The Apostles, *and* The Kingdom. London: Novello, 1900, 1903, 1906.

Kennedy, Michael. *Portrait of Elgar.* Oxford University Press, 1968.

Kistler, Jordan. *Arthur O'Shaughnessy, A Pre-Raphaelite Poet in the British Museum.* London and New York: Routledge, 2016.

Maclean, Charles. Review of *The Music Makers* in the *Zeitschrift der internationalen Musikgesellschaft*, December 1912.

McVeagh, Diana. *Elgar the Music Maker.* Woodbridge: The Boydell Press, 2007.

Moore, Jerrold Northrop. *Edward Elgar: A Creative Life.* Oxford University Press, 1987.

———*Edward Elgar: Letters of a Lifetime.* Oxford University Press, 1990.

———*Edward Elgar The Windflower Letters: Correspondence with Alice Caroline Stuart Wortley and her Family.* Oxford University Press, 1989.

———*Elgar: Child of Dreams.* London: Faber & Faber, 2004.

———*Elgar on Record: The Composer and the Gramophone.* London: Oxford University Press, 1974.

Moulton, Louise Chandler. *Arthur O'Shaughnessy: His Life and Work with Selections from his Poems.* London: Elkin Matthews & John Lane, 1894.

Newman, Ernest. 'Analytical Notes on *The Music Makers*', in *The Musical Times*, 1 September 1912, 566–570, reprinted in the programme for the first performance, Birmingham 1 October 1912, 9–17.

Odefey, Alexander. 'Edward Elgar and Gustav Mahler: The possibility of an encounter (part one)', in *The Elgar Society Journal*, 20/1 (2017); 'Edward Elgar and Gustav Mahler: "Who is virtually unknown in England" (part two)', in *The Elgar Society Journal*, 20/2 (2017), 17–37; 'Edward Elgar and Gustav Mahler: "The only man living who could do it" (part three)', in *The Elgar Society Journal*, 20/3 (2017), 25–50.

Pater, Walter. *The Renaissance: Studies in Art and Poetry,* revised edition. London and New York: Macmillan, 1888.

Porte, John, F. *Elgar and His Music: An Appreciative Study.* London: Sir Isaac Pitman & Sons Ltd, 1933.

Redwood, Christopher (ed.). *The Elgar Companion.* Ashbourne: Sequola Publishing, 1982.

Reed, William H. *Elgar as I Knew Him.* London: Victor Gollancz, 1936.

Rochlitz, Friedrich. *Sammlung vorzüglicher Gesangstücke.* Mainz: B. Schotts Söhne, 1838.

Rushton, Julian. *Elgar: 'Enigma' Variations.* Cambridge University Press, 1999.

———— '"How strange": Elgar's Early Notations for *The Black Knight*', in *The Elgar Society Journal*, 22/3 (2020), 5–11; 'Ballads and Demons: A context for *The Black Knight*', in *The Elgar Society Journal*, 22/4 (2021), 5–12; '*The Black Knight*: Elgar's First Symphony?' in *The Elgar Society Journal*, 22/5 (2021), 5–15.

Saremba, Meinhard. '"Unconnected with the schools"— Edward Elgar and Arthur Sullivan', in *The Elgar Society Journal*, 17/4 (2012).

Schubart, Christian Friedrich Daniel. *Ideen zu einer Aesthetik der Tonkunst.* Vienna, 1806.

Taylor, Benedict. *The Melody of Time: Music and Temporality in the Romantic Era.* Oxford University Press, 2016.

Thomson, Aidan, J. 'Unmaking *The Music Makers*', in *Elgar Studies*, ed. J.P.E. Harper-Scott and Julian Rushton. Cambridge University Press, 2007, 99–134.

Trowell, Brian. 'Elgar's Use of Literature', in Raymond Monk (ed.), *Edward Elgar: Music and Literature.* Aldershot: Scolar Press, 1993, 182–326.

Westwood-Brookes, Richard. *Elgar and the Press: A life in Newsprint.* Amazon [2019].

Whittington-Egan, Molly. *Arthur O'Shaughnessy: Music Makers.* Liverpool: The Bluecoat Press, 2013.

Young, David. *Beethoven Symphonies Revisited: Performance, Expression and Impact.* Brighton, Chicago, Toronto: Sussex Academic Press, 2021, 2022, 208–217.

Young, Percy, M. (ed.). *A Future for English Music and other Lectures by Edward Elgar: Peyton Professor of Music in the University of Birmingham.* London: Dennis Dobson, 1968.

Young, Percy, M. *Elgar O.M.: A Study of a Musician*, 2nd edition. London and New York: White Lion Publishers, 1973.

——*Letters to Nimrod: Edward Elgar to August Jaeger 1897–1908.* London: Dobson, 1965.

Unpublished:
Elgar, Alice. Diaries for 1911, 1912, 1913, transcribed by Martin Bird, with a note of explanation by Carice Elgar-Blake (prob. 1950s).

Authors Unknown:

'O'Shaughnessy, Arthur William Edgar (1844–1881)', *Encyclopaedia Britannica,* 10th edition. Edinburgh and London: Adam and Charles Black; London: The Times, 1902.

Reviews of the Birmingham Festival premiere of *The Music Makers*, in *The Musical Times* (November 1912), and of the Brighton Festival premiere, in *The Musical Times* (December 1912).

Printed in Great Britain
by Amazon

53049409R00097